One Lifetime–Two Lives!

One Lifetime–Two Lives!

Evelyn Aronson

ISBN-13: 9780692812556
ISBN-10: 0692812555

"Dedicated to the
Engaged Spectator
in all of us."

Acknowledgements

Let me explain how this book came to be.

It all started with skiing.

I don't ski. However, I am a professional at 'lodging.' Once a year our family would join my sister's family for a week of skiing in Snowmass, Colorado. And I would have this delicious time to be alone—with my thoughts. Some of these thoughts—about my life and about life in general (my 'philosophy-of-life' ideas)—were written down for future thinking.

Years later one of my daughters happened to find these notes tucked away in a drawer. "Where did these come from?" she asked. When I told her they came from her mother, she was rather surprised, but quickly recovered with, "Can I show these to the family?" Of course, that was fine with me. It's always good to get some attention.

The feedback I got was that what I had written was a little dry and maybe needed to be a more juicy read. Maybe I should not only try to communicate my ideas, but tell the story of how these ideas came to be. Even though this advice was coming from my children, it did sound pretty good. And the timing was perfect, as I had just retired.

So I have to thank my daughters, Rosy Aronson and Marilee Aronson; my husband, Neil Aronson; our son-in-law, Kim Aronson (our technical consultant); and our granddaughter, Maya Aronson, for their steadfast encouragement, support, and unrelenting pressure to transform my ponderings into a real book. But I would be amiss without special mention of the countless hours devoted by my daughter Rosy, who is the editor of the manuscript and the resolute guide through the obstacle course that is the publishing process.

This book is really a gift from my family. And I am very grateful.

Contents

Introduction

It suddenly dawned on me (like in the game of Jeopardy) that I finally knew the question. All my life I had been searching and exploring and coming up with different answers. But I never really understood the underlying question.

Now that I know the question, I want to share some of the answers that have crystallized for me over the years.

What I have written in the following pages begins like a personal memoir and follows a somewhat chronological path, showing how the answers formed—and are still forming—and, finally, confronting 'the' question:

What is the purpose of our lives?

In the words of Oscar Wilde, "Life is too important to be taken seriously." Also, it is too awesome to be taken for granted.

Yet our lives are sometimes buried in pain and suffering, completely extinguishing that 'joie de vivre.'

So then can we salvage any purpose? Must we merely endure until we die?

This is the challenge I have been grappling with since I was a young girl, witnessing suffering and yet feeling the joy and excitement of just being alive.

Without realizing it, I was leading two lives.

In fact, we all live twice.

On the one hand, we have our personal lives, our own stories, our own 'once-upon-a-times.' Some stories are happier than others. Some are longer than others. Some are easier than others. Each path is unique and unpredictable. We have only minimal control. We travel that path alone. And we travel that path only once.

But, beyond our personal lives, we have the gift of being able to experience *life* from a second perspective—more impersonal and universal. We cannot deny this other dimension. "I think. Therefore, I am." As soon as we become conscious of ourselves, we begin this double life.

I remember distinctly when our granddaughter looked in the mirror and said her name, "Maya...Maya...Maya." She was not only being Maya. She was seeing herself being Maya, from the newly acquired view of her second life, her life as a Spectator.

The essential human challenge, as I see it, is to be able to *enjoy life in spite of one's own life*—to somehow find purpose and rejoice in being alive through the bad parts as well as the good.

To meet this challenge I have been giving a lot of attention to exploring the potential of our second life—the life of the **Engaged Spectator**. I have come to believe that time spent on this level is like an insurance policy—because on this level life is ever-interesting and impersonal, and therefore protected from guilt, anger and personal pain.

In the course of my going back and forth between my two lives and spending a lot of time trying to make sense of my personal life by doing a lot of hanging out on the second level, I had time to do a lot of pondering. Because of the way my mind works, these ponderings had to all fit together—constructing what you might call an overall worldview based on examining and re-examining who we human beings really are. I would like to share this view as it seems to shed quite a bit of sunshine on my own personal path. And I would hope on yours.

Throughout our explorations I'd like to deal with certain basic questions, at least two of which we often dismiss as being merely theoretical. Perhaps a waste of time. And yet, consciously or unconsciously, these questions underlie much of our daily behavior. Really!

Whose fault is it?

Do we really have Freedom of Will (Choice)?

Is there a God?

Believe me, these questions do have every day consequences. And I think you will find them interesting to consider.

We will try to come up with *alternative* questions that can promote more understanding and harmony—both within us and between us. These questions will be basic themes running through the ensuing chapters.

Since we all live twice, I invite you to take time out from your personal life to just hang out with me in the second. Having two lives is totally awesome, something too good to ignore. As we contemplate life as a Spectator—an Engaged Spectator, just maybe we'll get somewhere in making the most of our personal journey. And in the process I believe that the ***purpose of our lives*** is naturally revealed.

In the following pages I'd like to take you along on my personal journey, not so much to create a memoir, but to trace the path of my ponderings. Let's call this venture a 'double-memoir,' telling the story of both of my lives.

I

The Little Girl in the Temple

I think I was always a 'good girl.' Nature? Nurture? I never remember feeling uncomfortable in my skin, or particularly jumpy, agitated, or angry (unless properly justified, of course). As far as I can remember, I was kind of shy and always seeking approval.

And maybe my opinion of my nature had a little outside help. My Mom and Dad always said I was a good girl. And I had no siblings to make me do terrible things to them. My mother thought I was so much better than she, and in my father's eyes, I could do no wrong. If you ever wondered what unconditional love could possibly mean, you should have met my father.

My dad was deeply religious, in what I consider the true sense of the word. He was loving, responsible, moral, and took great joy in the pleasure of living. His Jewishness had always given him direction and spiritual comfort—although not with strict adherence to 'the letter of the law.' So it was quite natural that, after our moving to a different neighborhood, he took on an active role in a newly established synagogue.

That's how I came to spend Friday evenings in a storefront temple with lots of approving adults (and hardly any children). And, being the 'good girl' that I felt I was, during the service I did what I thought I was supposed to do—namely, read the prayer book. I really did. And I took what I read—week after week—very seriously and without question.

Why am I choosing to start my 'double-memoir' here? Because this is where I believe my second life really began. This is where I have my first memories of my Spectator-self.

Thinking back, I can more clearly see why. I have become aware of the different kinds of prayers—prayers read and re-read every week—and the different kinds of insights that came with them. I'd like to present some of these prayers not for the sake of the prayers themselves, but only to consider their early influence.

But first, a rather important confession:

When I read the prayer book, I have always read rather selectively, picking out the parts that speak to me and blocking out the rest. This process has led to some interesting and perhaps controversial results.

For instance, the 'God concept' has been stretched to what some may consider unrecognizable dimensions. But more of that later...

What I want to talk about now is the strong impact of those Friday nights on my life journey.

As I sat there reading the prayer book (and occasionally thinking of Mrs. Goldberg's chocolate cake that came after the service), the constant repetition of these prayers, which I read very carefully each and every time, was having its effect. I was gradually becoming more and more aware of the world that existed beyond just me and of which I was a part. The ordinary components of daily life which could easily be taken for granted began to claim their rightful extraordinariness.

Let me quote an example of such a prayer. In an attempt to translate into language that is religiously neutral (applying my pick-and-choose methodology), I have made some minor substitutions, while hopefully leaving the essence intact.

"We are thankful ('We thank you, O God,') for this new day, for morning sun and evening star, for flowering tree and flowing tide, for life-giving rains and cooling breezes, for the earth's patient turning, the seasons' alternation, the cycle of growth and decay, of life and death....

May we come ('Help us, O God,') to see the wonder of being."

The effect of this kind of prayer officially put me in the role of the Spectator, seeing the world around me with a heightened awareness and sense of awe.

Another type of prayer, presented in abbreviated form, elaborated just what a 'good girl' was supposed to do.

"These are the obligations without measure, whose reward, too, is without measure:

> *to honor father and mother;*
> *to perform acts of loving kindness;*
> *to welcome the stranger;*
> *to visit the sick;*
> *to make peace when there is strife.*

Give us the courage to search for truth. Teach us the path to a better life. So shall we, by our lives and our labors, bring nearer to realization the great hope inherited from ages past, for a world transformed by liberty, justice, and peace."

As I look back, these prayers steered me in the direction of a social conscience and compassion.

The third example gives rise to the concept that we are all children sharing the same world and in some way responsible for each other. (At least this was my interpretation. You can choose to define 'God' in any way which works for you.)

"O God,(Spiritual Source?) the guide and inspiration of all humanity, You have spoken in a thousand tongues for all to hear. In every land and age, we, Your children, have heard your voice and imagined You in our separate ways. And yet, (O God,) You are One: though each may see You differently, You are the one God of all humanity."

And here began the understanding of the diversity and commonality of all these 'children.'

Such prayers and their myriad variations, which I have come to believe are actually embodied in some form in most modern spiritual teachings, became my first lessons in 'awe, morality and universality.' On Friday nights they seemed to go down especially well with milk and chocolate cake.

So, as far as I can tell, my personal search for the purpose and understanding of life unalterably began while sitting in temple those many years ago.

II

Everything Changes

It's Nobody's Fault

I mentioned being an only child. And that was true—until it wasn't. When I was nine-years-old, a wonderful thing happened: I had a new baby sister. She was everything I had always hoped for.

And my mother said, almost reproachfully, "We had her only because of you, because you wanted her." In her tone I darkly sensed a subliminal, "And it's your fault."

Fault? How could I possibly have been at fault? If anything, I should take pride in having had anything to do with such a perfectly divine happening.

But, being nine-years-old, I saw only the surface of things. And all too soon the surface began to crack.

You see, I was always loved and felt secure in that love. My mom was devoted to me, took good care of me, and things were fairly normal. Every once in awhile, though, she would seem to go 'off'—to kind of 'look for trouble,' to succeed in (from my perspective) picking a fight, screaming what a 'bad girl' I was, and stirring me into a complete wild frenzy. And there was the inevitable, "Wait 'til I tell your father."

I told you that I thought of myself as a 'good girl.' And this self concept almost magically seemed to provide a protective shell. Because whatever my mom said or did, I always knew that it wasn't my fault, and that, 'Daddy would understand.' Fortunately, he always did. He even managed to calm things down without making either my Mom or me lose face.

But somehow I knew that my mom was a little 'different.' Her mood swings could be quite scary. And my dad was dutifully in charge of making everything seem normal.

Until they weren't.

Having a second child proved too much for my mom. And she suddenly...'retired.' Her new responsibilities were overwhelming to her. She did less and less around the house. "Taking care of that baby is too much for me," she repeated in an almost accusatory tone. She was drained of all energy and motivation. More and more of the care-taking fell to my father. I have memories of him doing the dishes after dinner, sterilizing baby bottles and nipples, only to find we had run out of formula. I can still picture him frantically putting on his coat and going out into the dark, cold night on a desperate search.

My mother's 'off' moods became more frequent. She drew inward, more self-preoccupied and self-pitying. And my sister, instead of getting the love that I received, became the object of her resentment for the burdens and injustices she perceived to be her lot in life.

Over time the stress of making everything seem normal took a toll on my father. He would go through periods of severe depression and anger, mostly anger at himself for not being able to make everything right. However, that anger would sometimes spill over to my sister and myself, which would only make him more depressed and despairing. My father always thought of himself as someone who could 'take care of everything.' And usually he could. Except for those times when the cracks got too wide.

All this family stress was naturally having a big impact on how I viewed the world. While my earlier appreciation for the wonders of life never left me, making sense of the tumultuous storms engulfing our family became an immediate preoccupation. And I think, because of the worldview that came from sitting in temple and reading the prayer book, I began to more consciously experience my life on two levels.

First, of course, was the Personal level, worrying about what might happen that day. Would there be a big fight between my mother and my sister? Would my dad come home depressed? Would I do something to make things worse? Would there be more crying, suffering, feeling sorry...hoping? All this took place within the everyday life routines of school, friends—all that involved being 'Me.'

But I became increasingly aware of a second level—that level to which I could retreat and just watch. At that level, there was no sorrow, no judging—just the fascinating opportunity to kind of look and, just maybe, try to understand. It is this level I call the level of the Spectator, the level I first experienced while reading the prayer book on Friday nights. From this level one can indulge in just appreciating and studying what this life is all about—free from any pain, worry or suffering.

As a Spectator, I was finding new insights into what was going on in our family, and into human behavior, more generally. Being amply provided with an overabundance of material, I had a lot to observe. My observations resulted in a very unexpected conclusion, and one that completely altered my future relationships.

Assuming the role of the Spectator, I observed myself responding to our deteriorating situation in the way I had always perceived my father doing. I tried to make everything alright for everybody. That was the role model I had grown up with.

I would try to get my sister away from my mother when things got dicey. Lots of hugs and kisses. She was very cute. Then we would play games and make up weird delicious snacks. And I would spontaneously declare, "Honey, you're such a good girl and I love you so much." More kisses and hugs. They were too hard to resist.

And I was always playing defense, trying to do as much as possible so my mother wouldn't do something that might make her 'sick,' so that my father wouldn't come home to an unpleasant situation that he might be too tired to deal with in his usual wise and comforting way. I guess the label of co-dependent would fit pretty tight, psychologically speaking.

Being as honest with myself as possible, I really feel that I did the best I could. This family crisis situation was *not* **my fault**.

What about my sister? She was definitely innocent in all this. That's a no-brainer. She was an adorable, loving, bright little baby and little girl. She loved her daddy and me very much. However, when it came to her mother, it was a very different story. A power struggle evolved very early. The combination of our mother's resentment and attempt to assert her will over my sister, without the accompanying warmth and love, provoked strong resistance. Huge battles would occur over just taking a bath.

"You have to take a bath now." Those words would strike terror in my heart.

"Not now. I don't want to."

"You have to take a bath. You're all dirty."

"NO! Not now!"

"I said NOW!" Our mother's voice would take on a few decibels. She'd grab my sister's arm.

"I'm not going to!" At which point my sister would lie down on the floor and start to kick and scream.

"You bad girl!" And our mom would start to drag my sister toward the bathroom.

Who would eventually win out would vary, but in the end we would all lose.

The battlefronts multiplied: combing her hair, cleaning her room, and, later, "Practice your piano." And always, upon my sister's refusal, the unrelenting, "You're a bad girl."

Fortunately, early on my sister seemed to know it wasn't really her fault. Until the fights began to take on a new dimension. Our mother would work herself up to such a point that she would become 'sick' and lay on the couch for days, repeating the mantra, "It's all your fault," and, "I wish I were dead."

Eventually my father's pent-up frustration and pain would burst forth in the form of, "See what you've done. Why didn't you just take that bath?! Look at your mother now. It's all your fault!"

Now that's quite a power trip to lay on a very little girl. But I knew that my sister simply had no choice. She just couldn't take that bath. She couldn't give in. She inherently knew that, if she did give in to her mother, her spirit would be broken.

And so it was very clear to me that the situation was absolutely ***not* my sister's fault**.

But what about our mother? Wasn't she the guilty party? That's for sure. Wasn't she the grown-up? Wasn't she the one who had mastered, "The Parent's Guide: What *Not* to Do?"

Yes, what about our mother? This was the same mother that I had always known—the loving, adoring mother whom I had grown to love. But then I remembered more and more about those times when my mom had seemed to go 'off.' And how I carried this picture in my mind of our dad always caring for her, protecting her and making excuses for some of her questionable behavior.

Although our mom's irrational, hateful, damaging behavior toward my sister—and myself—enraged me, occasionally causing me to lash out in cruel, high-pitched rantings and ravings, somehow I could not completely blame her. Something compelled me to withhold judgment. I would suddenly find myself feeling this overwhelming pity for the mother that I loved.

Gradually I grew to understand more and more of what it was like to be our mother.

From what the years later revealed, I learned how our mom had always been a little 'different.' I heard stories about what sometimes happened when she was very young and sitting in her stroller. People would stop to talk to my grandmother. And my mother would start crying and shouting, "Don't laugh at me! Don't laugh at me!" Her memories of her own childhood were very negative. She was one of five children. "I was the one who had to do all the work. My brother was the favorite. I had only one doll, and he broke it." She didn't do well in school, and never developed a very positive self-image. She tended to be shy, brooding, and withdrawn. I'm sure my grandparents worried about her a lot and would have sought out professional psychological help if such a thing were accepted or easily attainable at the time.

My father met her at a party and fell immediately and deeply in love. She was very pretty and she was very sweet. But, from what I have deduced over time, he may have had reservations about her stability, as they waited fairly long before getting married.

They also waited long before having children. Taking care of me was about as daunting a task as my mom thought she could handle. When my sister was born, she decided she just couldn't handle it. She panicked. Like I said before, she just 'retired'—behind a barricade of blame, excuses, self-pity, and an ever-expanding armament of psychosomatic symptoms. Her defense mechanisms worked only against her, effectively keeping her from experiencing any positive reinforcement, any praise, any reason for self-satisfaction.

So now for the judgment part. It's easy to explain my sister's suffering, which could not be separated from the suffering of our father and myself, as our mother's 'fault.' But when you start to examine the circumstances of our mother's life and delve into the possible reasons for her actions, judgment becomes more problematic. Did she inflict our pain on purpose? Did she get any gain? *Could she have done differently?*

After all the questioning, I came to realize that our mom just did the best she could. Her defenses worked only to defeat her and deprive her of the love and esteem she needed so desperately.

And so, much to my surprise, it has become clearer and clearer to me that it was **not our mother's fault.**

Now what about our father?

Wasn't he accountable by not actively defending his daughter against her mother—by even venting his anger at my sister's expense, and thus adding to her burden of guilt? After all, he knew my sister had been unjustly provoked.

What *was* it like to be our father?

The image that has formed in my mind is of a man trapped between two loves. On the one hand, he saw his most precious little girl being mistreated and damaged by the wife he knew to be inadequate. But still he could not abandon his life partner whom he never ceased to love and to whom he had sworn 'to love and protect 'til death do you part.' So he valiantly strove to make everything right. And when the cracks multiplied and widened, his high expectations of himself dissolved into self-recrimination and a deepening sense of failure. He could not choose between his true loves, and thus was unable to save us from each other.

No. It was *not* **our father's fault.**

So whose fault was it? In the role of the Spectator, viewing from a calm vantage point above the emotional currents, it is possible to try a little alchemy—try to extract some illumination from the suffering of everyday life.

I came to the unexpected conclusion, after looking at our situation from each person's viewpoint, that **it was *nobody's* fault.**

And that, in dealing with one's fellow human beings, it is a luxury to simply judge. This all-too-tempting path leads past both understanding and solutions.

In the end, **it's *nobody's* fault!** This is the lesson I learned from my family. And this is the lesson that's essentially true in our everyday interactions with each other. However, this revelation goes against our obvious perceptions. Whose fault is it? Who is to blame? That's where a lot of our attention goes. And what I discovered growing up in my own dysfunctional family is that, **"It's *nobody's* fault."** This is one of the main themes of my writing—one of the reasons I decided to write this book.

But I'm getting ahead of myself. At this point I was too young to realize the full ramifications of my discovery.

III

The Ideal Attitude—at the Age of Eighteen

School life was busy and happy for the most part. Our mom would take pride in every accomplishment of mine, bragging to the point of embarrassment. Fortunately, her inflated opinion of her daughter balanced out my own tendency toward self-doubt.

(On the other hand, my sister's abilities were not similarly touted, and she lost out in any comparisons. In fact, "Can't you be more like your sister?" was the oft-repeated refrain. Actually, my sister's natural abilities and talents exceeded my own. But neither of us realized this until later. And I often reflect on how our lives would have been different if I were the second child.)

I graduated from grammar school with the distinction of being the only one wearing a matching arm cast, covered in the same aqua jersey as my dress. I had creatively fractured my wrist while dancing my way through the house and tripping over a desk. By the time the graduation ceremony was over, I had been successfully convinced by my family and friends how lucky I was to be so special.

High school also proved to be full and rewarding. I believe my Friday nights in temple when a little girl sharpened my curiosity. I took everything very seriously. Each new subject offered a lot to think about. In other words, a lot of my classmates found me weird. (To illustrate this weirdness, in college, if I didn't finish studying before a final, I would sometimes finish studying afterward.)

At home things alternated between the safety and more-than-occasional good times of the plateau and the inevitable descent into that abyss of family conflict, recrimination, tears, and the fear of impending disaster. And yet, while struggling in the darkness, I would find myself still able to rise to that other level and remain in touch with the world around me.

One memory in particular remains vivid. I was sitting in study hall looking out the window on a particularly beautiful, sunny spring day. Pale pink blossoms were gently swaying in the brilliant blue backdrop of sky. The image was breathtaking. And I started to cry.

The night before had been a nightmare, filled with mother's moaning, dad's angry despair, and the terrified sobs of my little sister. The Personal level of our lives was practically all consuming. Meanwhile Springtime's best show was being totally ignored, wasted. I knew it was impossible for my family to climb up to the Spectator's tower—at least at this time. And they were missing the marvelous show that is Spring. I was overcome with sadness. Our lives were eclipsing the blessings of Life.

My previous questioning continued to crystallize. On the one hand, the gift of life is such a miracle. Our bodies have such magical powers...to see and hear...to walk, run and dance...to love. We have the unique human quality of *consciousness* which enables us to explore all the diversity and marvels. And yet this same life is filled with constant challenges and tragedy...sickness (of mind and body)...war...natural disasters...and death.

Again, the essential question:

If the gift of life is wrapped in so much suffering, how can we fully enjoy its contents?

Many years later, I made an unexpected discovery. After managing for decades to successfully avoid more than superficial attempts to clean our basement, my husband and I finally ran out of excuses. Buried deep in the bottom of one of those countless boxes of 'treasures,' I found the speech I had written for my high school graduation. I was startled to find how much I still think like my very-much-younger me.

I'd like to include the speech, with some minor changes, because it ties together the strands of my thinking at the time.

The Ideal Attitude

"Graduation night provides the perfect opportunity for us to step out of our daily routines, to sit back, and to analyze.

Each of us has been blessed with the very greatest of all gifts, for we have life! And what a wonderful life it is, a mystery of beauty and opportunity.

In return for our rare gift, we face the fulfillment of an important obligation—the duty to make the most of this life.

It is a human tendency to judge life by each day's happenings. Often these incidents bring failure, discouragement, even tragedy; hence, the opinion that life itself is a series of disappointments, and certainly not the rosy picture of beauty and opportunity which I have just painted. But is this a fair judgment?

Day-to-day experiences taken at face value illustrate only the surface of life. It is by delving beneath this outer coating that we can find the true meaning, the great value of the miracle at our command.

To uncover our hidden blessings, to get the most of life, we must develop a rather challenging attitude which will raise us above the entanglement of everyday incidents so that we may evaluate life on its actual merits. This attitude must include three principal aims. I believe that by being specific tonight, by not speaking in generalizations, we can accomplish much toward establishing our own individual attitudes, which, of course, must vary.

The first of these is to harbor the desire to explore the physical aspects of life, to gain insight into the mystery surrounding the functioning of human life, to find out what kind of universe we live in, to find out some of the facts behind modern scientific miracles.

The second of our aims is to acquire a thirst for cultural knowledge. This is aided by acquiring a good command of English so that we can learn more, communicate, and eventually contribute. By reading good literature, history, and learning of other lands, other people, other times, we come in contact with many elements of life that we could never experience on our own.

Through our first two aims, knowledge of the physical and the cultural aspects of life, we become more aware of this life that we are living. And this understanding is all-important.

Let me show you why. Perhaps we buy a dress from the store. We enjoy wearing it, that's true. But let us suppose we make a dress ourselves. We understand its complexity and the work it represents—we then appreciate it all the more..and, as a result, we enjoy wearing the dress many times more than the store-bought one.

Can't we apply this to life? Through our first two aims we come to understand life, and through our understanding comes a deeper appreciation of our great gift. Conscious appreciation leads to truer enjoyment. Understanding, appreciation, enjoyment—this is making the most of life!

Let us now consider a third aim comprising what might be called the ideal attitude, fulfilling our basic goal of understanding. We must explore day-to-day happenings more fully than at surface value. Too often we take the good things for granted, paying little notice. Too often we let disappointments completely upset us and cause us to feel sorry for ourselves and to even sour on life.

But how to deal with disappointments—to somehow come up with a protective strategy? I have found that there can be some purpose, some meaning, in everything we encounter, even if we have to create that meaning ourselves. And in the search for it, we no longer see only the misdealing, but can actually come up with some redeeming aspects. (Though, one must admit, the search may be quite challenging.)

As a rather minor example of what I mean—several years ago our family took a trip South, following the directions given us by the Chicago Motor Club. We faithfully turned down Route 90, as the instructions directed, and proceeded for two hours down this route before we reached a startling conclusion. We were on the right road—but going in the wrong direction. We were very upset at our mistake and a good part of the day was ruined because of our poor spirits. However, after we had re-routed ourselves and finally accepted our situation, we realized that we were seeing many interesting and unexpected places that we would otherwise have missed had we taken the original route. We found that our trip had been much more worthwhile and enjoyable because we had taken the wrong route. Our error became a blessing in disguise.

The purpose behind a daily incident may be explained by what this experience has to teach us. Unfortunately, it is often through misfortune and failure that we develop strengths, insights, valuable character traits. The fact that some benefit is not always found does not mean it does not exist. It means only that we must look harder. (Remember, we are talking about an ideal attitude, one that cannot always be sustained, but one that we can strive toward.)

And so we have our three goals constituting the ideal attitude. It may be wise to periodically remind ourselves of these aims to keep them in mind. Let us remember:

- *the desire to understand the physical aspects of life;*
- *the desire to understand the cultural aspects of life;*
- *the desire to understand daily experiences in light of what they may offer for our personal lives and the understanding of life in general.*

Through such an attitude we are finding understanding, appreciation, enjoyment—we are making the most of life!

And, when we do come upon something that makes us appreciate and enjoy life all the more, let us take time out to say, "This is good. I am thankful."

Revisiting this speech, I was surprised to discover how much I was already struggling with questions of purpose and fulfillment in a world that is not necessarily user-friendly. Deeper reflection would have to wait.

IV

Caught in the Cross Currents

The College Years

I want to begin this chapter with a reminder that what you are reading is not truly a memoir. This book is not primarily about me or my family. This is about my family only insofar as my family has influenced my ideas and my way of looking at life. However, I do promise a more personal accounting a few chapters down the line. Meanwhile, we go on to the next stage, my college years, in a semi-personal, but—I hope—still 'juicy' narrative.

College was exciting from that very first day of high anxiety. I still remember waiting in line in a crowded Northwestern bookstore, surveying the scene, certain that each and every student was extremely confident and surely smarter than I. Never had I seen so many good-looking guys. And, true to Northwestern's reputation, the blue-eyed blond-haired female counterparts were drop-dead gorgeous. How would I ever fit in? Besides having brown hair, I immediately had visions of not being good enough, failing every test.

Fortunately, I was soon distracted from my feelings of inadequacy by the beauty of the campus itself, which lines Lake Michigan's lakefront. A walk from class-to-class could suddenly envelop you in a spectacular fall color show or a winter wonderland. Northwestern was far removed from Chicago's north side from which I commuted each day.

My classes soon took center-stage, benefitting from the wit and wisdom of some very dynamic professors. In a short time, involvement in the subject matter overtook my fear of failure. And I relaxed into the role of college student.

Looking back over my college years, two broad themes emerged: exposure to diversity and the search for commonality. Then there was the push-and-pull between idealism and reality. You might say I was caught in the cross currents.

Northwestern in those days was not noted for the diversity of its student body. It attracted students from all parts of the country, but basically the campus was 'White, Anglo-Saxon and Protestant.' I was part of a rather small Jewish contingent. But, with a little effort, it was possible to interact with a variety of people from different cultures, countries and age groups.

One experience I'm still smiling about was a dinner invitation from a Japanese graduate student who had become a good friend. Since I had never tasted Japanese food and my friend liked to cook, I gladly took him up on the offer. When the day finally came, my expectations of what a humble grad student's apartment looked like were confirmed as I entered the sparsely furnished and undecorated space. The 'floor' was attractively set with tablecloth and Japanese table settings, and the meal was a delicious assortment of dishes different than I had ever tasted. Feeling proud of my evident affinity for Japanese food, I showed no hesitation when asked, "Would you like some gravy?" "Of course," came the quick reply. My obliging host, much to my consternation, proceeded to crack a raw egg over my plate full of food. Trying to contain my visceral reaction, I valiantly ate everything on the plate, all the while struggling to maintain a pleasant demeanor and uninterrupted conversation.

I had many more delicious meals at my friend's, but I never again asked for gravy.

My classes, naturally, were the main source of diversity, constantly opening up new ways of thinking and new things to think about. A terrific freshman requirement was a year-long course in human development that included trimesters in psychology, sociology and anthropology. Also required was a fabulous course in English literature, fortunately taught by a nationally well-known 'professor-entertainer.' Then there was this outstanding professor in biology.

As an aside, it's hard for me to understand the standard college curriculum of today. When our oldest daughter registered for her first year, she was given a huge book and told to select her courses. There seemed to be no basic core requirements. Especially in a country as diverse as ours, doesn't it seem important to transmit a basic understanding of our cultural heritage and the physical world we live in? If one pursues primarily career-based studies, upon graduation is one truly 'educated'?

This, in turn, brings up a central question: What does it mean to be 'truly educated'? My understanding of this term was also caught in the cross currents—taking a real buffeting in the next four years.

Prejudice—on Campus?!

Perhaps the areas of study to which I felt a more personal connection were those of psychology, philosophy and comparative religion. And, of course, literature embodies all three. Some of the books from these courses I cannot part with, and these books still occupy major space on our basement shelves and *cannot* be moved. My husband has his own permanent collection. When I think about it, these shelves contain books which, even if rarely looked at, have formed part of my husband's and my own very identities. They reflect who we are—and discarding them feels like discarding parts of ourselves.

I would like to take the time to go over some of the main ideas I took away from the three favorite subjects mentioned above, namely psychology, philosophy, and comparative religion.

First, **psychology**. My family history gave the formal study of psychology immediate importance. As we would study new concepts...defense mechanisms, self-image, projection, superego...my inner ear would hear, "That's my mom!"; or, "So that's why my sister did that."

While these concepts apply to individuals and help us to understand their differences, they also represent general principles of human behavior which apply to all of us, regardless of one's country, social class, or color of skin. Diversity and commonality—point and counterpoint.

Following this line of thought, I just took for granted that college students who studied psychology, sociology and anthropology became 'educated.' I expected my classmates to start to question prior prejudices, try to interact with others differently, as individuals, beyond the old generalizations and stereotypes.

This was my assumption. But such assumption was dramatically undermined by something that occurred in my junior year.

This is what happened. I was taking a course in economics, which was equally interesting and difficult. My professor, most distinguished-looking and brilliant, was from a Nigerian royal family (actually!). I referred to him as the 'African prince.' After class, I would more than occasionally need to ask a question. My questions began to extend beyond the day's content to his country and his political views.

On a couple of occasions our discussions continued over a cup of coffee. I found him fascinating. We talked about all sorts of things. I was especially intrigued about his personal history, his 'royal' background, and the intertwining factors leading up to his becoming a professor at Northwestern.

One day while I was studying in the student union, a friend came up and asked if he could talk with me in private. In private?! What could that possibly be about? He needed money? Women troubles? He was gay? (Actually, in those times, homosexuality never entered our conversations.) Lots of intriguing scenarios ran through my mind, but none prepared me for the conversation that followed.

"Evelyn, you're pretty happy here. Right? You have good friends. You're dating a lot of the boys in our club. So, as one of your friends, I want to tell you that I'm concerned."

"Concerned? About what?"

"You know, some of us have seen you with that black professor. And, while it's probably fine, you know how people talk."

"That's right. I do see him. He's quite amazing."

"Well, that's probably true. And *I'm* really not prejudiced. But you know how some people are. I hear comments. And I just felt I should warn you. You really should stop seeing him. Or other people might stop seeing you. You know what I mean?"

I could hardly speak. What I was hearing came as a total shock. I respected this friend—and his friends. And I assumed that the courses we were all taking were really change agents.

An old saying comes to mind, "You can lead a horse to water, but you can't make him drink." And I would add, "If he does drink, you can't make sure *what* he is drinking." So it is with knowledge. What you experience is filtered through the prism that is you—formed by heredity, family, society...and chance.

Here was a bright student, good-natured and, obviously, a caring friend. Yet, at least in this case, his openness to learning was disappointingly limited. It certainly didn't seem to result in a positive change in behavior.

It was then I realized that one can graduate from college not really 'educated.' Basic unexamined attitudes can remain basically unexamined—barring some fortuitous event or inspiring teacher. The disillusionment of that day remains with me.

Oh, No!—Not Philosophy!

Two other favorite courses I mentioned earlier were **philosophy** and **comparative religion**. My instant connection is easily traced to the 'girl in the temple' reading about the world that existed beyond just her. The questions I had been absorbed with since then were the actual content of these subjects. A quotation from Bertrand Russell's *The Problems of Philosophy* states the value of philosophy in a way surprisingly similar to my own point of view.

> *"Philosophy, if it cannot answer so many questions as we could wish, has at least the power of asking questions which increase the interest of the world, and show the strangeness and wonder lying just below the surface even in the commonest things of daily life."*

To me, philosophy's ultimate goal is to expand our consciousness.

One of the most gripping mysteries of a baby's growth is the emergence of consciousness. As mentioned in the Introduction, I remember that sense of the miraculous when our granddaughter became self-aware, voicing her name for the first time. "Maya...Maya..." she kept repeating, beaming with self-satisfaction.

Consciousness is what makes us unique. Other creatures share the same needs—food, sustainable environment, reproduction. But we alone have the gift of consciousness. And with consciousness comes a compelling curiosity. Watching a baby staring intently at everything and everyone is truly engaging. Answering the questions of a toddler, a young child reveals the depth and breadth of their wonderings.

I saved a letter my friend wrote:

"...Jacob, our oldest, is now six and one-half. He is our sensitive little southern gentleman. Sometimes I have to remind myself he's only six...especially when he starts wondering about the universe and asking me those really hard-to-answer questions. For example, today the classroom hamster died and he was just crushed. Our evening meal was then punctuated with questions like, "Where is heaven, mom? Is it above the clouds or someplace in your heart?"

But somehow this curiosity dims and, without notice, the familiar fails to fascinate and is taken for granted. Our consciousness, rather than continuing to expand, becomes preoccupied with the everyday challenges and pleasures which make up our personal lives.

And yet the consciousness of that six-year-old yearned to soar, to contemplate the mysteries of our existence. He was already a student of philosophy, starting to ask those basic questions, questions which human beings alone have the privilege to ask:

What is the nature of reality?

What is truth?

What is goodness?

What is beauty?

How do we know?

In all likelihood little Jacob may stop asking these questions much too soon.

The fact that these questions do not occupy more of our everyday discourse never ceases to amaze me. Philosophy was not a popular subject and is an endangered species on many college campuses today. My interest was definitely not the usual. Yet I have trouble understanding how these questions can be ignored.

Maybe we don't really ignore and avoid these questions. We just relegate them to the realm of religion, which attempts to provide answers. But by doing so, we can face a central problem. Namely, that many religions start with the answers and make a pre-emptive strike on the questions. They often require strict adherence to prevailing doctrine. So that we stop asking our own questions and give up our personal adventure of discovery. (And besides, what if the answers are wrong?!)

Which brings us to the study of comparative religion.

As I mentioned, I approached this subject from a Jewish perspective. Fortunately, from my point of view, my religious upbringing was not 'orthodox.' Within Judaism there is a broad spectrum of practice. My early religious studies led me to believe that the search for truth was never-ending and imperative—no matter where that search might lead. Religion and philosophy were natural partners.

The diversity of belief systems introduced in our course was mind-boggling, as we explored Christianity in its various forms, Islam, and the religions of the East. Each system had its very distinctive underlying philosophy and ritual. My innate compulsion to seek commonality, however, resulted in a concentration on their similarities.

The origins of practically every great religion can be traced to outstanding individuals, whether through reason or revelation, dealing with a similar set of existential questions:

What is the purpose of life?

How do we relate to the unpredictability and fear of nature's power?

How can we overcome suffering?

How do we face death?

How can man be made 'good'?

Most importantly, religion reflects a universal spirituality—an inborn sense of awe and reverence—a recognition of the transcendent power of Being. There seems to be a religious 'instinct' that cannot be denied. Every culture has a religious component—if the definition of religion is generously interpreted.

For me, Judaism provides its own answers to man's basic questions. It has much to contribute as one very important path to 'climb the mountain' to a good, purposeful life. Other paths beckon with their own rich landscapes. To be able to mine for riches is indeed a privilege. And that college class in comparative religion extended that privilege to me.

The Ugly American

After my junior year, I was unprepared for another memorable bout of disillusionment, especially since it occurred as a side effect of a very great opportunity.

I came home from campus one day and casually told my parents that I had heard about a very reasonable student tour to Europe that summer. Little did I expect my dad's reply.

"Why don't you go?!"

"Go? Who, me? You must be kidding!"

"Why not?"

"Dad, it's a lot of money. (It was about $800, including food, lodging, and transportation!) And who would go with me? None of my friends, I'm sure. I just mentioned the trip to give you a little campus news. And now you sound serious..."

"I *am* serious. Europe. So much history. So much culture. A wonderful adventure. We can come up with the money."

"But, Dad, you wouldn't want me to go by myself...to a foreign country, all alone."

"Why not? You'll be fine."

(This was in keeping with my dad's seemingly unshakable faith in me. And his own unquenchable delight in learning.)

And so it was that summer I set off on a student tour with young people from all parts of the country. By the time we left, I was totally excited. When we got to Paris, our first stop, we were met by a German bus driver who accompanied us throughout the trip. In each new country we were introduced to a new student guide from that country. The group was not too big. We had been provided an ideal way to travel.

Amid the excitement of meeting the French, the English, Italians and Austrians, I had (here comes the disillusionment) the unfortunate experience of encountering 'the ugly American.' The students I was with were all going to be college seniors. After three years of a supposed college education, I observed the kind of behavior I had heard about but never quite believed. To give an example: our student group would walk into a restaurant and, before too long, would begin to make a public display of their aversion to the local cuisine, demanding we leave and go for "good American food," while making sure these demands would be overheard by everyone in the restaurant.

Another thing I found difficult to accept: when the day's touring was over, my fellow travelers would spend evenings writing letters and washing under-wear—remaining totally indifferent to what was going on in the bustling streets outside.

Perhaps the most illuminating experience for me happened in Germany. One of my trip-mates was a Jewish New Yorker. Being in Germany was understandably traumatic for him, haunted by the memories of the Holocaust (although he, himself, had lost no close members of his family). His conclusions were formed before we even entered the country. He found nothing positive. He saw only 'the German people'—whom he regarded with suspicion and intense dislike.

In contrast, our guide was Austrian. He spoke of his personal suffering at the hands of the Russian occupiers during World War II. As a child, he was of-ten hungry, cold and mistreated. I asked, "Don't you hate the Russians?" He seemed taken aback by my question. Thoughtfully he replied, "There was this one Russian soldier who secretly gave me food and watched out for me. He was my friend. How could I hate 'the Russians'?"

Now this Austrian is my idea of an 'educated' person. He saw beyond the stereotypes. To me, he mastered the essence of what psychology has to teach. He related individual to individual.

Political Activism and the Selfish Gene

Keeping in mind my overall positive college memories, there is one more area which fell below expectations. Somehow I just assumed the lively class dis-cussions in history, political science and comparative governments were gen-erating this desire to participate, to make our own society better. With the presidential elections coming in November, we had our chance. Some of us would be voting for the first time. After all, we were living in a real-life de-mocracy—no small piece of change.

At first, political activism did seem alive and well on campus as preparations for the much heralded mock political convention got in full swing. This mock convention was a celebrated tradition at Northwestern, held during every presidential election campaign. Multiple committees, posters, banners, editorials and debates played out an elaborate overture to the main event. After this tremendous show of effort and commitment, the winning candidate was...no other than BEN HOGAN, the champion golfer. To my sad disappointment, in this mock political convention, the emphasis was on the 'mock.'

To make an understatement, most college students at that time didn't take politics seriously. They didn't exactly base their self-image on their role as 'citizen.'

Why do I bring up the self-image? Well, this political lethargy was really bothering me (and still does). But around this time, we happened to be studying a very interesting concept in psychology that diluted my frustration with some understanding. (Righteous indignation is not easily given up.) This concept revolved around the self-image. In our psych classes much attention was being paid to this self-image. One particular theory has stayed with me all this time. I came to think of it as the *evolution of the 'self.'* Let me explain.

The basic assumption is that we all pursue our own self interest. Let us accept the fact that: **We are all really selfish.** (Actually, this is one of the main themes of my writing.) There is nothing to debate or to apologize for. Let's face it. *Being 'selfish' is a natural consequence of our basic instinct to survive.*

The more important question is not *if* we are 'selfish' (because we necessarily must be), but *how do we define that 'self'?*

As a baby, the sense of self is all *'Me.'* That's all there is. Later one can identify with *'My Family.'* Succeeding stages become more and more optional. Some of us feel strongly about *'My Community.'* Or *'My Team.'* Or *'My Religion.'* Then there can be passionate identification with *'My Country.'*

And, as globalism has become an inescapable part of our everyday, more and more individuals connect to '**My World**.' Whatever is incorporated into one's self-image demands loyalty and dedication.

As a dramatic example, in World War II young men willingly fought and died for their country. Were their actions purely unselfish? Let's think about that a little more. Weren't they really fighting for '*My Country?*' Upon further reflection, it seems they were actually pursuing their own self-interest—which in no way diminishes their actions or their heroism.

To me, a truly educated person, living in a democracy, would have an expanded self-image. '*My Interest*' would include those of *Myself, My Family, My Community, My Country* and *My World.*

Taken to a practical level, being politically active—to try to make one's country better—is merely acting in one's own self-interest. And so the evolution of the self-image leads naturally to the **ENGAGED Spectator**. More of this later.

To summarize my college years, I was caught in the cross currents of 'idealism' and 'reality'— the exposure to diversity and the search for the common threads that bind. I am still caught in those cross currents.

V

The Explorer in Training

Teaching

In this chapter I want to tell you about some of my most memorable teaching experiences. Even if you are not a teacher, as former students, parents, and grandparents, we can all easily relate. Besides, this is not only about teaching. This is about what teaching taught me.

Ever since I can remember I always wanted to be a teacher. Or maybe a nurse. Those were the most popular choices for a woman when I went to college. Fortunately for me, either choice fit perfectly.

After graduation I took on the role of 'first-grade teacher' in a progressive suburban school, fully supported by the administration and community. It was a middle-class neighborhood, but not at the wealthy end. The school atmosphere was fairly relaxed and informal, giving the green light to creativity in the classroom.

Now was my chance to test out the college theories in the laboratory of a real school. The results were often expected and even more often surprising.

Needless to say, the first day of teaching found me very excited and nervous. In fact, I never really got over the excitement and the nervousness. I still have those recurring dreams where it's the first day of school and I can't find my classroom, have no idea what I'm supposed to teach, and am panicky and unprepared. But the truth is I loved to teach. And I'm glad I started 'in the beginning.'

First grade is a wonderful time. Curiosity is at its peak and the teacher can do no wrong. Those bright trusting eyes looking up at you light up the classroom each morning. So much opportunity...and so much responsibility.

The Teaching of Reading and the Self -Image

I taught before the age of computers. The modern classroom is completely different now. These days, many children start learning to read in preschool or kindergarten. Also, technology has produced a broad range of tools to aid in the individualization of instruction. But I would like to take you back to the 'olden days' to show how what was a problem then is still a problem today, but one that may not get the attention it deserves.

One of the first challenges I encountered came with the teaching of reading: how to set up reading groups. (In those days only one or two children, if any, came to first grade knowing how to read.) The standard procedure was to form small groups in terms of ability. Sounds logical, right? Except I just couldn't do it.

My college psych courses (so essential for teachers) had made me acutely aware of the effect of early experiences on the self-image. How could I label someone a 'Robin' (smart one!) or a 'Bluebird'? "If you give different names, the kids won't know..." The kids know *every*thing—especially when the Robins fly through the first book and land on the second.

In first grade, self-images are ripening and extremely vulnerable. Children come together from a variety of backgrounds and exposure. Their potential is still a mystery. Premature labeling can damage that potential. This was my challenge.

I decided to experiment teaching reading with the class as a whole and then breaking into small groups, encouraging the more advanced to buddy-up and help their partners. This was a win-win. The more advanced students felt very good about helping their buddies. Besides, they were stimulated with supplemental reading and special projects. (Today the computer opens up a whole new world of choices!) Those having trouble keeping up had extra instruction by me or their buddies, without the stigma of a label. Their confidence in tact, they could freely explore their other abilities.

I know that new teaching techniques and technology offer much potential to enhance and individualize learning. But, with all the choices and emphasis on achievement, we must always remember that what must be nourished, above all, is a child's self-image. That will never change.

Introducing the Explorer
Alias the Engaged Spectator

Even beyond the teaching of basic skills, I felt my main goal was to imbue students with a permanent *love of learning*. The image of an 'explorer' took hold in my mind. An explorer represents to me someone on a life-long journey in pursuit of new experiences and new ideas. I began to see this 'explorer' concept as a central part of my teaching. It became an unconscious and then a conscious goal to get each child to see himself/herself as an **Explorer.**

(Looking back, I can see I was aiming even higher—to raise them to the level of the Engaged Spectator. But more of this later.)

I started out the year by teaching "The Explorer's Song." I can still picture little Alisa and Russell, standing so serious in front of the world globe, proudly singing their song—with all the motions, of course.

The Explorer's Song

Who am I? Who am I?
Why, *I'm* an *Explorer*!
What do I do? What do I do?
Well, here's my "Explorer's Song":

The world is full of wondrous places.
Inner, outer, 'on-ner' spaces.
To *see*, to *hear*,
To *touch*, to *smell*—
I'm off to see the world!

To further build on the Explorer's theme, magnifying glasses were always liberally distributed throughout the classroom. Often the kids felt compelled to bring in assorted 'discoveries' (usually of the creepy, crawly variety) to make sure the magnifying glasses were sufficiently utilized.

Every year there was The Pet. What else can spark a child's curiosity and affection like a little fellow creature? Just for fun, I'd like to digress a bit and share some of our pet stories.

We started slowly, with the usual goldfish, and then progressed from turtles, chameleons, to lively, brilliantly-colored parakeets. Then there was the year of the beautiful white mouse. This was surely the best yet, until I could no longer deny the questionable smell greeting me each morning as I opened the classroom door. The mouse, regrettably, was a school dropout that year.

Next the ants came marching in—in their ant farm. And then were the times when the ants chanced to march *outside* the farm, and we all had to do 'round-up'!

This reminds me of a romantic story, about the first time my future husband came to the house to meet my family. When he walked in, we were in the middle of a family crisis. The ant farm, having moved to our home for summer vacation, had toppled off the dining room table. Ants were crawling everywhere. Upon entering, Neil's first impression was of our family on hands and knees frantically pursuing the escaping ants. We could tell he was one of us when he joined us down on the floor and soon proved his ant-retrieving skills.

But the grand finale was a pair of garter snakes, which the kids lovingly named Cookie and Snookie. These visitors were most cooperative playmates. Little hands would often reach into the water-free aquarium home to take them on short classroom excursions. The kids made sure the snakes' home was cleaned, and our guests were fed regularly with special turtle food.

Now for the climax of this cozy tale. At parent-teacher conferences I often invited the children to participate. During one of these conferences, Ilene was playing with Snookie, taking him on a tour of the classroom, while I was talking with her mother. Suddenly, out of the corner of my eye, I saw Snookie start to gyrate in wider and wider circles until...WANG! It took a dive for Ilene's arm, and mouth connected to skin! I bolted up, snatched the errant snake, and tossed it back into the aquarium, firmly replacing the lid. Upon immediate examination it seemed that Ilene suffered no serious wounds, but we decided it would be wise to take her to the emergency room anyway. I must have looked so upset that Ilene's mom (with whom, luckily, I had always had a good relationship) seemed even more worried about me—repeating over and over that it wasn't my fault and that Ilene would be fine (which thankfully, it turned out, she was).

To tell the truth, it *was* my fault. You see, snakes don't eat turtle food. They actually require live offerings, like mice. I was unknowingly starving poor Snookie to death.

I shall always be grateful to Ilene's mom for her support when anger (and lawsuit!) was the more normal response.

Shortly after this episode, and before I had had the chance to relocate them properly, Snookie and Cookie mysteriously disappeared from their home. An all-school alert followed. After days of a futile search, Cookie was found in the cafeteria dishwasher. Snookie was never found. The kindergarten teacher refused to eat in the school cafeteria from that day on. And so ended the Year of the Snake.

A big part of our explorer's theme was a trip up the evolutionary ladder, which formed our year-long science curriculum. "But first, in order to understand the world we see, we must find the world we can not see." So we discovered molecules through experimenting with air, heat and crystal formation. Then we turned to one-celled organisms, analyzing drops of water under the microscope, watching the miraculous movements of these microscopic beings. "Cells came together in many new ways so that animals could do more and more things." We studied the arms of starfish, looked for the lateral sensory lines of fish, watched tadpoles develop, touched the interlocking barbs of feathers, compared types of fur (hair), all the while looking for similarities and differences in appearance and function.

One goal of our evolutionary trip was to appreciate just how wonderful *our* bodies are. A little 'experiment' the kids loved was very simple. I would hold up my fist in front of class and say, in a most commanding tone, "Second finger, rise!" Most amazingly, the second finger would rise! "How did that happen?!" I would ask. And indeed the kids looked like they had seen a miracle. (*And they had...*)

Each species that we studied was honored with its own song and its own pictures to be colored. And each student went home to teach his parents the songs and experiments, so they could be good explorers, too.

To me, a highlight of our year's study came with Dr. Seuss' blessing. From the famous *Green Eggs and Ham* comes the exhortation, slightly modified:

"You do not like it.
So you say.

Try it! Try it!
And you may.
Try it and you may, I say."

To be good explorers, I wanted my kids to be open to new and unfamiliar experiences, to challenge themselves to go a little 'beyond.'

Here's where the chicken stomachs come in. In studying birds, we talked about how birds swallow their food whole and chew with their stomachs. How better to connect words with reality than to poke around in the contents of a chicken's stomach and *see* what it eats and what happens to it. As an antidote to the inevitable "Yuck!," and the groans and the grimacing, I endlessly repeated the above refrain.

And for reinforcement I called upon *The Little Engine That Could* with its encouraging:

"I think I can...I think I can...I think I can..."

With this strong back-up, practically every kid succeeded in swallowing his/her initial revulsion and bravely sticking out his/her little pinky and poking around inside that chicken stomach, ending the experiment beaming with the triumph of being *a real explorer.*

Reflecting back on my years of teaching, I have found the concept of an Explorer to be very effective. Identifying as an Explorer can actually alter a child's self-image, generating a genuine curiosity and a pride in learning and discovery. It's quite exciting to watch this happen.

Upon further thinking, aren't we all explorers on a journey through life, wanting to make this journey as full and rich as possible? And isn't school the place to jump-start that journey?

'Compassionate Spectator' Training

The term 'real explorer' took on new meanings with each additional year of teaching—especially after an incident that is indelibly fixed in my mind. It was then I became focused on a missing component in my definition of 'explorer,' and in what I was attempting to instill in my students.

I was out in the playground on recess duty one cold winter day when some of the kids rushed over. Tugging on my coat and pulling me forward, they repeated, "Hurry, Mrs. Aronson! Hurry! They're fighting! They're fighting!"

And then I saw two of my students in all-out-combat. As I looked on in temporary paralysis, our class bully, Lance, had knocked his weaker partner to the ground and was proceeding to pound his victim's head into the ground. Fortunately, my paralysis was short-lived, and I was able to intervene in time to prevent any serious injury.

Here was a little first-grader acting out our collective instinct for violence—with no trace of restraint or compassion. To this day I am haunted by this image. *All our lofty ideals for peace—for justice—actually hang on what happens to the first-graders of the world.* Nations act no differently than the human beings they represent. What happens to Lance, and to all other children, has worldwide consequences. I ask myself to this day, *can this instinct for blind aggression somehow be controlled and redirected?* In our never-ending pursuit of peace, this is the guiding question.

So, to my theme of Explorer (the Spectator), I realized I had to add a new dimension (Compassionate). While this sounds pretentious, I had no grandiose expectations and was actually thinking in very simple, concrete terms. Some form of *'compassion training'* came to mind. And what might 'compassion training' be?

Is there a recipe for cooking up a little empathy? Fortunately, more and more cookbooks are being written on this subject. Following some of these recipes, I started to devote more time to talking about feelings...how we *feel* when things happen to us.

Like..."How did you feel when Bobby wouldn't let you play with him at recess?" Or, "What makes you angry?...Sad?...Scared?" Perhaps becoming more aware of others' feelings and *how similar they are to our own* might heighten awareness of the needs of others—and, just perhaps, stir some compassion into the mix. Besides, how can that hurt?!

At this point I would like to interject an interesting technique that someone once shared with me and which has never ceased to intrigue. Conflict resolution is a very important part of a teacher's job description, and that's no small part. So whenever two students got very, very mad at each other, I would try my experiment. I would propose that each one shake hands with the other *while looking each other straight in the eye*. And, if they did finally agree to do it, when they looked directly into each other's eyes, something quite magical happened. They would gradually begin to smile, and even laugh. And suddenly the anger and hurt dissolved and it was like they couldn't remember what was such a big deal in the first place. I often wondered if, as they looked into each other's eyes, they saw their common humanity.

In graduate school I had the wonderful opportunity to take a course with Dr. Bruno Bettelheim, an internationally-known professor of psychology. Something he said always stuck in my mind and would resurface whenever an incident such as that with Lance occurred. Dr. Bettelheim's mantra was that, no matter what you were teaching, you must immediately stop everything and deal with real-life problems when they come up. *These were the really important teachable moments.* With Dr. Bettelheim's words always in my mind, I did try to do that as much as possible.

The Golden Rules

And so evolved the Golden Rules for 'real explorers' (the third rule being dedicated to 'compassion-training,' of course):

I. *Be a good Explorer.*

"The world is full of wondrous places..."

II. *Try your best*...and, no matter what happens, feel good about yourself.

"I think I can...I think I can...I think I can...

"I'll try it. Maybe I'll like it."

III. *Do good deeds.*

Help each other. Remember, *we're all the same inside.*

To illustrate this last point comes another tool in "compassion training." This attention-getting experiment can have dramatic effect. In front of the class, I would take an open scissors in my right hand and hold up my left. With a sudden sharp movement, I would aim the scissors toward my own upheld hand—taking enough time to appreciate the looks of disbelief and alarm on the faces of my little audience. Not to worry, I would manage to just escape contact.

I would continue with my intended moral, "Remember, if you stick any one of us with a scissors (or a bad word), we *all* feel pain. (And at appropriate times I might add, "...no matter if we're black, white, or green; fat or skinny; smart or not so smart...) We're all pretty much the same inside.

On the other hand, if you do or say something nice to any one of us, we *all* feel good. (And so do you...) We're all the same inside.

I have found these 'Golden Rules' to serve as my main blueprint for teaching. They may have developed in a first-grade classroom, but, I must admit, they summarize my own philosophy of life. And they incorporate for me the main principles of the Engaged Spectator.

My No-Fault Theory of Education

(Remember: It's Nobody's Fault!)

It has become steadily clearer to me that *what* is taught (the basic subject matter) cannot be divorced from *how* we teach it. And how we teach depends a lot on our underlying view of human behavior.

This brings us back to the problem of Lance. Realistically the attitudes and behavior we foster in the classroom can have only a limited impact on Lance—although this influence should not be undervalued. However, while in the classroom, how a teacher teaches depends a lot on how they interpret their students' behavior.

So here is where my view of human nature comes in. Psychology classes and daily living brought me to view personality and behavior as the product of multiple factors intertwining in ever new combinations to create the Lance I saw each day. Factors of environment and heredity played their shell game, daring me to find who or what's to blame for Lance's misdeeds.

When I started teaching, I admit to a bias. I was all-too-ready to blame the parents when it came to a child like Lance—constantly demanding attention, defying authority. So when I met his mom and dad at conferences, I zeroed in on the father's critical attitude toward his son, an unusually intense power struggle between them, and the father's denial of any trouble. The parents (in this case, mostly the father) were surely the problem.

Then again, there was Rachel, initially hostile and emotionally unavailable. To understand her, one had to see her in the context of the community. Her parents had moved into this suburb to better Rachel's opportunities. But they had limited means and couldn't 'keep up with the Joneses.' Rachel became resentful of all the things her classmates had that she didn't. She began to feel quite inferior. Her parents, very aware of their sacrifices in order to put their daughter in this 'better' school, were increasingly angry with her ingratitude. Their lack of understanding was definitely a big part of Ruthie's problem. Again, the verdict went against the parents.

But there was something wrong with my initial picture. The brush strokes were too thick. The more contact I had with the parents, the more I came to realize that, even though I could see how their actions might not be serving their children's best interests, *most parents were genuinely trying their best to be good parents.*

What I'm afraid I too often overlooked was the influence of heredity. In the environment-versus-heredity debate, my college training came down pretty strong on the side of the environment, which is a pretty good side to take as a teacher. Every child can learn; every child can achieve as long as the teacher tries hard enough. That sounded pretty good, until Kyle walked into my classroom.

Kyle was small, adorable, and very pliant. He sat quietly in reading group, demanding no special attention. There was only one problem: he wasn't learning to read. I began almost daily tutoring during lunch and/or after school. His reading buddy gave him extra time. The parents followed through with lessons at home. But, as the year progressed, Kyle fell further and further behind. I finally had to accept the fact that—contrary to the popular concept of 'No Child Left Behind'—some children will be left behind in specific areas. Heredity will claim its due. (This, of course, does not get us off the hook from pushing the Kyles to their full potential, finding areas where they can excel, and guarding their feelings of self-worth).

Having children of my own sure changed my tune in the environment-heredity tug-of-war. Heredity suddenly took center stage. I was now the vulnerable parent, defensively pontificating, "You can't blame the parents." I saw first-hand how kids come pre-packaged. Ability-wise they're different. Emotionally, they vary so widely. Some are cute; others are, honestly, not. When you visit a hospital nursery, you see babies sleeping peacefully like little angels. Others are flailing about, wailing at the top of their little lungs. And this is before the environment (post birth) has had much opportunity to enter the scene.

In conclusion, you can't put all the blame on the parents. You can't blame the child either. (He/she's just a child!) You can't even blame the teacher (who seems to be getting most of the blame these days). Remember, 'it's nobody's fault.' (To quote myself, "Multiple factors in constant interplay determine behavior.")

However, this in no way releases the parents, the child, or the teacher from responsibility for his/her actions. But when that responsibility is not exercised, it is more useful to look for causes rather than to assign blame. Thus I would like to illustrate my 'No-Fault Theory of Education.'

Let's use Lance as an example.

Mrs. Green, one of the other teachers he worked with, was always telling me, "He's so bad. And he's lazy, too." The energy she directed toward him was usually somewhat negative and punitive. Her interaction reinforced his already negative self-concept, encouraging him to act even 'badder.' Understanding his behavior was not her strong suit. "He's just a bad boy. His problems are his own fault." Therefore, she was off the hook.

But she was avoiding the mystery lurking there. I eventually came to realize something that is obviously so obvious. ("Elementary, my dear Watson.") Each child, although sharing the same classroom experiences, is, of course, traveling with their own baggage. I can see only the outside. Every classroom needs nothing other than a Sherlock Holmes to pry open the lock and peek inside—just enough for clues how best to reach him/her.

Although not a Sherlock Holmes, I did uncover some clues about Lance at parent conferences. I got to know more about his home situation. The clues pointed, among other things, to a troubling inability to control his actions (perhaps to some extent genetically based), feeding a negative self-image. Detective Aronson plotted a new approach. *To focus on fault seemed irrelevant.* What I could do is try my best each day to be positive, patient, but also firm. I constantly altered my responses to meet Lance's changing moods and needs, attempting to arrange situations where he could have positive interactions with his fellow classmates. I worked with his parents to help them build a more constructive image of their son. Eventually, the detective work seemed to yield some results. I think Lance began to feel I cared. Gradually there was a growing feeling of trust, even an occasional sign of affection. He started to show enough *self*-trust to work through a new concept, rather than his usual giving up in rageful frustration. And he was beginning to relate to his classmates in a more favorable way.

Would this progress continue? Would his self-image develop in a positive direction? (Or, in more Shakespearean terms, would he grow up on the side of man's *humanity* to man?) No one can know.

But by not dwelling on blame and accepting one's own responsibility, at least a teacher can try to open the door to change and healing.

No Simple Answers
Looking from the Outside In

After looking at education from inside the classroom (from the inside out), I'd like to consider how society looks at the classroom (from the outside in).

While I realize I am getting further away from my actual classroom experiences, as a former teacher I feel personally involved in the daunting challenges for the teaching profession today and for education in general. And I think you, too, face similar concerns.

So let us don the role of the Engaged Spectator and continue our considerations.

Although most adults in our country have children of their own, you would never know it listening to the public debate on education.

"We need more discipline. That's what's wrong with kids today." Probably a statement from a parent having plenty of trouble controlling his/her own kid's behavior.

"Schools don't need more money. They already have plenty. They just waste it. If you just don't throw more money at them, they'll figure it out..." From a parent whose school district is overcrowded, understaffed, under-equipped, in physical disrepair—and who has just voted down a school referendum.

"Parents are not doing their job." From a citizen who denies the obvious fact that many children grow up today in dysfunctional or broken families, or, in many cases, with no families at all.

I once attended a school board meeting discussing class-size limits. The board was made up of mostly businessmen. One board member, arguing for raising the number of children per classroom, showed a chart basing class numbers on the actual physical dimensions of the room!

At a time when America is losing ground in the race to keep our students competitive in an increasingly global economy, we are desperately seeking simple solutions: accountability (translation: tests, tests, and more tests); higher expectations; strict standards; merit pay; school vouchers—all of which require no major reassessment of our country's priorities and *no major investment of resources in public education.*

As a fairly typical example of the media's 'sound-bite' solutions, I read an op-ed piece in the New York Times entitled, "*Why School Achievement Misses the Poor.*"

The columnist referred to a California education think tank Ed Source survey which listed the top factors for a "higher-achieving school": (1) lofty expectations for all students; (2) clear, measurable goals; (3) a consistent curriculum; (4) and a staff that pores over data to see where teachers and students can improve. His main point, well taken, is that high-poverty schools are far more likely to be staffed by low-quality, less-qualified teachers.

He continues, "The studies keep coming that show that schools can raise student achievement with stoic principles and dedicated teachers who toil in a 'shared culture' against all odds."

But just what are those odds? And why don't those odds get the media and/or the political spotlight?

In all fairness, the author did add to his top factors for a higher-achieving school, "Such schools have teachers who are not only willing to push students, *but also come armed with up-to-date textbooks and other resources*"—a slightly important addendum, I would think.

The majority of teachers and principals, while initially entering their professions wanting to do a good job, are not capable of sustained "toil...against all odds." As in any profession, you have many outstanding individuals, but most are not that exceptional, although they might wish to be. For a majority, the odds beat them down and their goal becomes survival. Even the superstars eventually reach 'burn out'—as they toil against those often overwhelming odds.

Teachers and educators have become the scapegoats for the larger failures of society crying out for attention. The spotlight is not on the 'minor' factors, such as poverty, unemployment, dysfunctional (and under-supported) families, drugs, lack of funding or health issues that impede our children's learning. The spotlight is on the teacher.

As an aside, I often ask myself if I would choose to be a teacher today. As far as I can see, much of the fun has been taken away. You can't even hug your students for fear of a lawsuit. Creativity has been replaced with testing and strict external objectives. There is less time—or no time—for gym, art, and music. Students often have little chance to let off steam and be 'available for learning.' While recess and lunch periods get squeezed, and a longer school day is being called for, there is less down time to plan and recharge for teachers. (The students have less time to recharge, also.) *And* it's harder to make a decent living—especially when compared to other, more lucrative professions.

One more thing: how do you keep up your morale when blame is your constant reward?

For instance, as mentioned above, there is a shrill chorus of accusations that it is teachers' prejudice toward minorities that result in low expectations and/or indifference. Hence, the education gaps.

While prejudice can and does play some part in educators' failings, such accusations are targeted even at school systems where there has been a recognition and a concentrated effort to deal with such prejudice.

The Evanston school system is one such district. Evanston, a suburb of Chicago, has long prided itself on its diverse population. There is a high percentage of African-Americans, both middle-class and fully integrated into the community (and academically performing at a comparable level with other middle-class students), and lower-class, largely in neighborhoods where housing is cheaper.

Over the decades the Evanston school system has experimented exhaustively to eliminate the disparities between the 'white' and African-American students' academic achievement. A busing system was introduced to ensure that each school within the district had a similar proportion of white and African-American students. Teachers were trained in a color-blind philosophy. The community fully supported the district's efforts, including the willingness to back school policies with tax dollars.

Yet the gaps did not disappear, and accusations of discrimination still, decades later, provide a constant drumbeat. But this is a school district where there *is* a 'shared culture,' and dedicated principals and teachers *do* toil against all odds. An effective debate about education must confront just how complex and daunting are those odds.

Such a debate must include a deeper look into three major obstacles facing our schools today, namely: *poverty, cultural differences,* and *psychological factors.* Not the stuff of media sound bites. But their full significance is unbelievably overlooked in today's cookie-cutter approach. So let the force be with us as we continue our search for answers.

Poverty has far more power to alter a child's school performance than a teacher's attitude. Children come to school hungry. They suffer from the effects of drugs, Aids, alcohol and violence. Resulting birth defects and poor medical care take a further toll. Parents may be absent or unwilling or unable to provide care or support—let alone enrichment. My friend teaches in a poorer district in Milwaukee. She called a child's home in frustration after a day of particular academic lethargy and disruptive behavior. From the other end of the phone came the reply, "Well, you really should know, Johnny's brother got shot last night. And he died." That might account for some lack of concentration.

Cultural differences, when considering the probability of academic success, must be squarely confronted and not hidden under the false cover of political correctness.

The difficulties of overcoming cultural barriers to academic success were personally demonstrated to me when my mother became very ill. We hired a caretaker, Juanita, who was very sweet and devoted. As to her background, she had almost no education as a young child in Mexico. By the age of twenty-five, she was the mother of four, all born in the United States. My dad went out of his way to provide Juanita and her children with a background of new experiences, taking them to the library, talking about history, encouraging reading, buying tickets to the ballet. But in their home they continued to watch only Spanish-speaking TV and listen to Latino music, and they showed little interest in absorbing more of the American culture. (In fact, I sensed a resistance—a fear of betraying the pride and deep connection they felt toward their own heritage—a feeling that we were looking down at their values and way of life.) When asked about goals for the future, the girls were quite content with their family life and talked only of having families themselves. Although they were poor and experienced first-hand the dangers of living in an inner-city environment, they showed little interest in pursuing higher education as a means of bettering their lives.

Juanita's husband, however, was extremely frustrated. He knew what it was like to struggle to make a living without a special skill or a high school or college degree. Yet the immediate culture in which his family was growing up did not support his ambitions for his children. Their closest role models— parents, family, friends—valued hard work and family, but did not present examples of academic or economic success to be emulated.

Let's take a look at another sub-culture. The disconnect between African-American culture and 'mainstream' America is, in some cases, as complete as between neighboring countries. Despite the wealth of rhetoric, relatively little effort has gone into studying, *feeling* what it is really like growing up 'black' in America. And no amount of blame and/or shame can make up for the need to really understand the unique complexities of this separate culture in order to unlock the doors to educational achievement.

The challenges of cultural differences in motivating and integrating students cannot be ignored. However, now, when private and charter schools are becoming more the norm—and public schools are increasingly home to those on the lower rungs of the economic scale, there is less opportunity for this cultural understanding and integration. Ironically, now more than ever, *the importance of a strong system of public education* calls out loud and strong. It is an essential component in uniting our differences into "one nation, indivisible—with liberty and justice for all."

A third major factor in determining academic success is a child's **psychological readiness**. Today more and more children are being raised without the support of a stable family. Divorce, both parents working, single parenting, frequent moves, separation from extended families, all add an extra dimension to children's stress levels. Psychological needs are often invisible when society looks from the outside in.

Just because a child is in the classroom, he/she is not necessarily *'available for learning.'* While it is definitely true that the schools must be held accountable for their major role in shaping our future generations, to blame the school system as if isolated from the larger society is a serious misdiagnosis. If we are truly sincere about education being our nation's priority, then our society as a whole must be held accountable. In public discussion of education, the problems of *poverty, cultural obstacles*, and *psychological stresses* should be front and center. It's not just the teacher.

When our understanding of our schools from the *outside in* comes closer to the view from the *inside out*, we may find the will and the ways to more realistically support our schools—and our children. We cannot escape responsibility by blaming the student, the parents, the school. We must come to understand the multiple factors contributing to a positive learning environment and, as a society, work toward turning those factors in our children's favor. The schools are a reflection of the society they serve. Building better schools requires nothing less than a major investment in building a better society. *There are no simple—or cheap—answers.*

In truth, we are all teachers. Teaching is a partnership of school, parents, and society dedicated to training real explorers to lead us into a brighter future.

At the beginning of this chapter I wrote about teaching as an opportunity to test out the college theories in the real world of the classroom. We've come a long way in our reflections. I think my main conclusion, which we really knew at the onset, is that teaching children is so much more complex than any theories—although a good teacher should be well-grounded in theory.

Teaching is not just the transmission of knowledge and/or skills. Teaching is all about attitude. As I see it, the main goal of teaching is to create a permanent love of learning, a desire to be a *'real explorer.'*

An *explorer-in-training* has 'brain tapes' implanted which play over and over: "I think I can...I think I can," and "I'll try it. Maybe I'll like it."

He/she becomes a Spectator, one who can impersonally observe life with a deep appreciation and wonder.

He/she becomes a Compassionate, Engaged Spectator, one who recognizes that, basically, we're all the same inside. And this recognition creates a desire to help, 'to do good deeds,' to make the world better.

(Sounds like a description of a pretty good grown-up. Doesn't it?!)

VI

Graduate School and Freedom of Will

The Anatomy of a Decision

I am not going to devote much time to my personal experiences in graduate school. But one memory stands out as having dramatically altered the way I view human behavior—and, ultimately, the way I make the choices I do. To put it in a more practical way, I learned *why* 'it's not my fault!'

My new insight at the time, believe it or not, had everything to do with *freedom of will*.

Most of us do not spend much time wondering, "Do we really have free will?" B-o-r-i-n-g... We even avoid such questioning as being of little or no practical value. But the truth is that each of us *has* formed our own unique answer, and that answer—usually operating below the conscious level—does deeply affect our daily lives and the everyday choices we make. This realization has had a profound effect on my understanding of just how we come to make the choices we do. But I'm getting ahead of myself. Back to graduate school.

I enrolled in a master's degree program at the University of Chicago after I had already begun teaching. (My teaching was very much affected as a result.) As mentioned earlier, I had the enviable privilege to have as my professor Dr. Bruno Bettelheim in a course named The Atypical Child. I had heard a great deal about Dr. Bettelheim, whose work was known world-wide. He was a Holocaust survivor and, during his long and illustrious career, came up with some very original and controversial theories about human behavior, no doubt majorly influenced by the trauma he endured during the war. Over the years, his reputation has been challenged. However, regardless of how history will come to judge him or his work, I, for one, can testify that he was the most impactful teacher I have ever had (and I am fortunate to have had some very impressive teachers).

Entering his classroom each day was a challenge in itself. You never knew if you would find the kindliest grandfather figure, smiling ever-so-genuinely, determined to impart such wisdom as to sweeten your life permanently—or the angry, arrogant taskmaster waiting to inflict the latest round of punishment to chisel away at life's hidden teachings.

I remember an incident during a lecture one day when a misguided student timidly suggested that our imperious professor might have erred in his citing of a specific date in history. From that day forward our fellow classmate became the target of continual abuse in a campaign to reduce his stature in our eyes to a zero-minus. This event, you can safely bet, severely limited questions and comments from the rest of us, giving the dear Doctor front-stage-and-center access at all times.

But, yes, I did say he *was* a great teacher, if you were willing to pay the price of admission. One of his techniques was to pick certain students to represent different stereotypes through which he illustrated the various points of his lessons. For example, I became the 'naive suburban school teacher' far removed from real-life experience. So when I did summon up the courage to ask a question, by the time he received it, twisted it around to his liking, and threw it back, it seemed indeed the question of a naive lightweight. However, after he was done making me look sufficiently foolish, I had to admit he had succeeded in making his teaching point crystal-clear.

After class my friends would rush up to me, sympathetically inquiring, "Are you alright?! Are you alright?!" And I would manage to answer, "I'm fine." And that was indeed true, but only after I had taken a step back and realized that what was dished out was not personal. I could see that I was merely a necessary tool in what I considered to be a painful yet effective teaching technique.

I always felt that Dr. Bettelheim was driven by a deep concern that we teachers were missing out on teaching's deeper potential—which he was earnestly, relentlessly trying to communicate.

One of Dr. Bettelheim's memorable themes (which was referred to already in the previous chapter, but bears repeating) still remains a guiding principle for me.

The dear Doctor painted the following scenario for a teacher:

"The weekly curriculum requires completing two chapters in the social studies text. You see your goal within reach—but you are also aware of a serious bullying incident that occurred at recess immediately before class. Should you continue with the lesson and deal with the incident later, and then only with the two students involved?"

The 'naive suburban teacher' (my role!) would, of course, be set up to agree with this plan—prompting the Doctor's utter dismay.

"And what is the real purpose of teaching?!" he would righteously bellow. *"To teach about life and how to live.* You drop everything and teach the lesson that presents itself. Of course it's a lesson for the whole class!"

I have tried to carry this lesson into my personal life. I find that, when I'm busy pursuing a planned schedule and 'life happens,' I sometimes remind myself that maybe it's a good idea to 'drop everything' and deal with life's improvised agenda.

Another main theme high on Dr. Bettelheim's list was the fostering of creativity. As an extreme example, he told the story of a little German girl who lived through the bombings in Berlin during World War II. As time went on, tragically they became more of a routine happening.

One day she surprised her mother with an innocent observation, "Oh, mommy. Sometimes I think I'm so lucky. I get to see trees fly!" Here was the ultimate (and creative!) Spectator.

What is the 'Anatomy of a Decision?'

Now let's get back to that particular lesson in Dr. Bettelheim's class which had a permanent impact on my Spectator's view of human behavior. This lesson generated some very important questions: Do we actually have 'freedom of will' (or, interchangeably, 'freedom of choice')? Or, basically, what's behind the choices we make? *Why* do we do the things we do?

Trying to answer these questions led to what I call my theory of "The Anatomy of a Decision"—with some some very surprising conclusions.

Dr. Bettelheim provided a classic illustration that will help us look at how we actually make our decisions:

> *Picture yourself driving on the expressway and you are late for an appointment. How would you control your foot's relationship to the gas pedal? How fast would you decide to go?*

Through this simple situation, Dr. Bettelheim proceeded to highlight the entire process of decision-making. He began with the assumption that our self-image places us at differing points on a multitude of continuums. If you rate yourself fairly high on the continuum of 'being on time,' and take pride in always being punctual, your foot would get heavier on the pedal. But then, if you also have a high rating on the 'law-abiding citizen' scale, the current speed limit would suddenly sound an alarm. Spontaneously your foot would ease up on that pedal.

Where those two continuums (among many others) intersect at any given moment will determine the changing pressure exerted by a very tenuous foot-pedal relationship. And thus the 'choice' of how fast to go would be made, and we have partially dissected the anatomy of a decision.

By implication, every action we take is the result of an infinite number of intersecting factors coming together at the very moment of decision, only a very few of which are we conscious of.

Dr. Bettelheim's assertions inevitably lead to the basic question of free will. After all, given the above description of the way decisions are made, are we really in control of our actions?!

To approach this major question openly and in the spirit of empirical inquiry, let's try to put aside pre-existing ideas or religious implications. For now, let's just simply take our analysis step-by-step.

Using Dr. Bettelheim's approach to the dissecting of a decision, looking still deeper into the 'anatomy of a decision,' let's focus on the self-image.

I believe it is really our self-image which determines our present positions on the various continuums. Then what determines our self-image? Now we get into more complex terrain. What is necessary is major digging in the areas of *genetics* and *environment* as played out in the dimensions of *time* and *place*.

Whoa! This sounds heavy. But for the sake of illustration, we can make it simple. In fact, to make this exploration a little sweeter, let's start with a piece of chocolate.

The decision will be: to eat—or not to eat—that extra piece of chocolate.

While this may sound like a trivial decision, it easily relates to more serious ones—in fact, to every decision we make.

First, let's introduce the *genetic* component. I have personally witnessed an *innate* affinity for 'sweets.' When I became a first-time mother, I conscientiously avoided all contact between our daughter and any obvious form of the 'S' word to keep her free of that sweet addiction. One day we were at the checkout counter of the supermarket and, before I could intervene, the cashier put a lollipop into a plump little open hand. It was love at first 'lick'—no need to acquire a taste. My daughter had claimed her inheritance.

It follows that our genetic inheritance, unique to each of us, demands constant recognition.

The whole process of *environmental* conditioning cannot be overstated. Our entire family seems to share a love of sweets. While this may taste of genetics, *cultural* factors cannot be overlooked. The menu is read from the bottom up. Holiday parties celebrate the joy of eating dessert. And, traditionally in the Jewish culture, the dessert table has been more popular than the bar.

The environment also sends complex, changing messages which all claim their due impact at the crucial moment of 'decision.' What about the health factor constantly spotlighted by the media—and the dentist? And the peer pressure to look slim and trim? And the TV and magazine ads that make chocolate so irresistible?

All these messages are being received at a very *personal* level. The way people receive these messages are determined by their own personal history and landscape.

So which of these messages will bounce off the mountains of resistance and which will find a receptive landing place? A lot will depend on your ever-fluctuating *self-image* (getting back to our starting point), which is exquisitely sensitive to genetic and environmental factors.

How do you view yourself on the continuums of 'self control'; 'positive body image'; 'intelligence'; 'health consciousness'; 'adaptability'; 'religiousness'; 'self love'? And that view may change on a rainy day, or when you are tired or sick, etc., etc.

And now we must add the dimensions of *time* and *place*. Are you hungry? Are you feeling especially good about yourself today? Is everyone else eating that extra piece of chocolate? Will your host be hurt if you don't? Will everyone 'look down on you' if you do?...

So now is the time of decision.

(What follows may sound complicated and may be hard to accept. But it underlies much of what my writing is all about. So I ask you to go along and try to relate what I am saying to how you actually experience your life.)

Looking into the microscope: Your decision will be decided by the sum of all the factors interacting at the exact moment of decision: genetic, environmental, personal, time and place. ***You have no choice.***

But you *must* choose.

You will *consciously* be aware of making the choice of whether to eat that chocolate (or take that job, vote for that candidate, go to church, compliment your spouse, stand up to your boss, talk to or punish your child...). Whether or not you believe in free will, you will make the choice.

And you will feel you are deliberately making that choice because: To *experience* choice (or free will) is inherent in human nature.

Choice is inescapable. (And so is *responsibility* for our choices—which is something we will deal with shortly.)

You cannot decide not to choose, for that is a decision.

However, although we consciously *experience* the act of choosing, our decisions are the product of a complex process. It's really not simply 'our choice.' (It also follows that the results of our decisions are not simply 'our fault.')

Although this sounds confusing, the explanation comes from something we have been talking about all along. We are now taking advantage of having two lives! And this is a perfect illustration of the value of using both of our lives.

In our Personal life, we experience having control over our choices. This is undeniable. However, our Spectator-self is aware of the underlying anatomy of our decisions. There is a big difference in how we view life's happenings from our Personal perspective and how we see things from the view of our Spectator-self. And there are differing consequences from which perspective we take.

So now we are ready to deal with these consequences— with why this whole business of choice is so important. Why has this question raised in Dr. Bettelheim's class those many years ago refused to be sidelined in my curious psyche? Why do I feel the whole issue of freedom of choice is so relevant in our daily lives and not just the impractical indulgence for the philosophical mind?

Because I think that by understanding the *process* of choice, (the underlying anatomy of our decisions), we can make better choices, for ourselves—and as a society.

So how does this actually work? Putting our theory into practice, let's return to our decision of whether or not to eat that extra piece of chocolate. (While I realize this may not be the most important decision we may make today, it continues to provide a sweet and easy example.)

Let's say the moment of decision has now passed and you did eat that chocolate. As this nugget of pure pleasure (perhaps milk chocolate filled with creamy caramel and cashews...) deliciously melted in your mouth, you knew you made the right decision.

But almost immediately the pure pleasure became bittersweet, diluted with the after-taste of guilt. And now you feel you made the 'wrong' choice.

Here is where 'the anatomy of a decision' comes into play. Depending on your understanding of how choices are made, different interpretations and consequences will follow. Let's demonstrate by describing two possible types of interpretations:

Interpretation I: The Personal response (our usual immediate response)

Interpretation II: The Spectator's response (suspending judgment)

Why do I call Interpretation I the 'Personal'? Because that's the way Evelyn Aronson might usually respond. However, if I'm lucky (with a little time to reflect), my Spectator-self might take over with a bit more objectivity.

So back to the business at hand.

The Act: You eat the chocolate.

Interpretation I: (The Personal)
I have complete freedom of will. I made the choice.

Self-**Interpretation:**
"I ate the chocolate. I'm guilty. I'm weak. It's my fault. I don't like myself."

Other-**Interpretation:**
"They chose to eat the chocolate. It's their choice; it's their fault. No wonder they complain about their weight. I don't feel sorry for them. They brought it on themselves."

Comment: We have just witnessed a new dose of internal and external negatives added to an ever-evolving self-image. And the result? The added guilt will probably make it more difficult to resist that chocolate next time. The factors in the equation affecting future choices have been altered—and not for the better.

~

Interpretation II: (The Spectator)
My 'choice' is the sum of all factors interacting at the moment of decision.

Self-Interpretation:
"I ate the chocolate. But I'm not guilty. There are reasons. Maybe it was alright to eat it this time. I was hungry. I needed a little sweetness in my life today. I didn't want to offend my host. Or maybe it was not right. Then *why* did I do it? Maybe I was tired. Maybe I wasn't liking myself so much today. Next time I'll try to be more careful."

Other-Interpretation:
"They ate the chocolate. It's not their 'fault.' I can't judge them. I don't know the many reasons for what they do. *Is there anything in my behavior that has or can—or should—influence them? (Like maybe not offering it to them next time.)*

~

I believe that Interpretation I is our very favorite and is the natural response. *Since we personally experience freedom of choice, we feel we should be able to control our behavior.* And if someone does 'wrong,' we assume we/they are guilty and deserve to be blamed/punished.

"She's lazy."

"He's bad."

"It was their choice."

"I have no will power."

It's her fault. It's his fault. It's my fault!

However, viewing our decisions from Interpretation II, our Spectator's perspective, we go beyond guilt and blame. We can suspend judgment, seek understanding.

I have to say that this perspective completely changes the way we look at the actions of others—and our own! I cannot emphasize enough how different things look from the view of our Spectator-self. It's a good practice to try viewing things from your second life more and more. It's really quite interesting analyzing the possible reasons for behavior. (Even if this analysis comes after the behavior, it's still a good exercise—just like our yoga!)

There is another perhaps unexpected consequence to looking at things from both of our lives that I think is necessary to deal with. This is our 'common sense' attitude about our ability to change our own behavior. I have come to believe that: **We cannot change our own behavior.**

What?! Now that really makes no sense!

But let's take the time to think this through more carefully. Most often a person is unable to change themselves no matter how much they want to. And no matter how much we expect them to. *The underlying factors have not changed.* And this is a very important point—one that is very difficult to accept.

Dr. Bettelheim attempted to understand the process of choice in a way similar to a physicist trying to determine the path of a ball, by analyzing the different factors impinging upon it—and within it. Unless those factors are altered, the ball will continue its course.

We do know how difficult it is for us to change a 'bad' habit. And how angry we can be at ourselves for our inability to change.

But behavior can and does change. The factors determining our decisions change. Our daily contacts, our physical condition, our self-image is always changing. The downside is that we cannot *consciously* control those factors.

My friend told me of the problem she had controlling her weight. She tried diet after diet. She consulted with professionals. Nothing helped. Then one day her family doctor looked at her and said, "You're obese." Somehow that word set off alarm bells that had previously been silent. And her behavior actually changed.

We often need a little nudge, a change of circumstances, a little outside boost. We need to judge less and encourage more—and that includes ourselves as well as others. Sometimes it is only outside influences—from others or the larger society, or just chance—that can trigger better choices.

Now I'd like to take this discussion from the individual level to a broader consideration of the consequences of our different interpretations.

Just a quick glance at the daily news sources or an innocent eavesdropping on casual conversation shows just how much of our daily conversation is devoted to finding out who to blame and/or the act of blaming itself. I and others call it the Blame Game.

But when we put our decisions under the microscope, the 'anatomy of a decision' reveals *it's nobody's fault!!!* The whole concept of 'fault' is a dangerous detour from trying to take constructive control over our decisions and our actions.

The concept of 'fault' is the natural outcome of viewing our behavior from Interpretation I. "We make our own choices." (We have freedom of will). But there are serious consequences to this interpretation.

For one thing: *It lets the 'other' (or society) off the hook.* If it's somebody's fault, then we have no responsibility toward them. "The Lord helps those who help themselves. So why don't they?" (We really don't have to bother with the *why*.)

A second consequence: *It limits our ability to change behavior—our behavior and the behavior of others.* Once we figure out whose fault it is, there is often no perceived need to analyze what happened and seek to alter those factors causing the undesirable actions. Plus, we don't even have to feel sorry for the 'guilty' party—unless it's us!

In a previous chapter on my teaching experiences, I tell the story of Lance, a 'problem child' who could easily be written off as 'lazy,' 'selfish' and 'bad' by his teacher—and his parents. However, looking for the 'why' of his behavior can uncover clues to bringing about a more positive Lance.

There is a third consequence I'd like to bring up, one that has benefitted me personally in a big-time way. When I look at people through a 'no-fault' lens, it makes it easier for me to tolerate their behavior, if not change it. Now that *is* an important benefit! You don't get so mad. You don't take things so personally. It's harder for someone to 'push your buttons' because *you're* not the problem. If your husband doesn't ask directions (which we find is a trait shared by many of the male gender), you may be able to reduce your irritation to a slow boil.

One very important misconception of a 'no-fault' interpretation is that people are not held accountable or punished for their actions. After all, "It's not their fault." This is absolutely not true. Society could not exist without holding people responsible for their actions. The goal is not to excuse people for their actions or prevent their dealing with the consequences. The goal is to make those consequences optimal for individuals and those around them.

Let's apply our 'no-fault' perspective to real-life consequences in today's society. Our criminal justice system provides a case in point.

Let's take what happens to Steve, a drug dealer—not a major player but an active street player. He must go to jail—no 'ifs,' 'buts' about it—to protect his community. But taking the time and effort to study the possible causes leading to his crime might suggest a different set of consequences more beneficial for him and society in general.

As many others in his neighborhood, our hypothetical Steve was raised in a dysfunctional family where lack of money, alcohol and abuse were primary ingredients. His school had limited resources and peer pressure channeled him away from academic efforts. Employment opportunities for young people ranged from slim to none. Furthermore, he had no particular skills, and any job he might get would be at minimum wage with no benefits. Finally, he was given the choice of pushing drugs—with lucrative rewards—or facing peer rejection and even physical retaliation. There is one more thing to be mentioned. Based on observation and the comments of family and friends, he was basically a good kid with a high learning curve.

Steve definitely must go to jail. But what happens to him there?

In spite of scientific studies indicating other objectively desirable alternatives, society has rallied more and more around "Interpretation I."

"Steve sold those drugs. He's guilty. He deserves to be punished. We've got to teach him, and others, a lesson—once and for all!" ('Tough on crime'—a great campaign slogan!)

But what's the lesson? The prisons are overcrowded and understaffed. ('Warehousing' I believe is the current lingo.) Sounds like perfect conditions for teaching worthlessness, hopelessness, and resentment toward the society of which he is definitely not a part—lessons he has already learned too well.

And what can we expect to profit or learn from our huge investment in a burgeoning prison industry (besides the money generated from businesses and jobs that might otherwise be directed to education, solving our energy crisis, and/or competing in a global market, etc.)? The prisons are still crowded with repeat offenders. The rate of recidivism is proof that intended lessons are *not* being learned.

An alternative approach (Interpretation II) would take into account the factors that produced the criminal behavior. Prisons could become 're-entry stations' providing training, education, drug treatment, psychological resources, jobs, and an invitation to become a bona fide member of mainstream society. Fortunately these ideas are more recently gaining traction and starting to replace the 'tough on crime' attitudes which have prevailed. (Of course, many prisoners are beyond rehabilitation or their crimes too heinous. But today's prisons are filled with men and women like Steve who would welcome a better way—who would gladly 'pull themselves up by their own bootstraps' if society would give them just a little boost.)

Back to a more personal level, to appreciate the difference between a 'fault or no-fault' perspective, I play a game with myself. When I find I'm reacting to what someone does—or when I'm reacting to some news event—and I experience the pleasure of self-righteous blame and indignation, I try to switch to Interpretation II. "What could have made her do such a thing?" "*Why* do they hate America so?" It's like the air goes out of the balloon. The rush to anger is considerably slowed. The black and white fades into questioning gray.

On an even more personal level, once I realized 'it was not my mother's fault,' it became so much easier to live with her—and love her. And, on the other hand, feeling loved and accepted, it was possible for her to love me.

Before concluding this discussion I think I need to address some underlying concerns. I am not dealing with the existential issues of whether or not our actions are predetermined. That is not the subject of this discussion. I am focusing only on what cannot be denied: that choices are determined by the sum total of factors interacting at that moment of decision. We have no real control. On the other hand: to *experience* choice (or freedom of will) is inherent in the human condition. It is also part of the human condition to bear responsibility for one's choices and their consequences—even though, 'It's nobody's fault.'

When I refrain from assigning fault, I refuse to be dismissively labeled as a 'bleeding-heart do-gooder'—although, I do admit to a compassion addiction. (And I do admit that understanding more fully another person's situation does often evoke compassion--and even admiration.) My main purpose is not to excuse bad behavior, but to focus attention less on blame and punishment and more on understanding this behavior. I believe that by studying 'the anatomy of our decisions' we can come closer to our goal of making 'better' decisions—with better consequences for us, and for our society.

What are the 'right questions?'

I would like to close this chapter by searching for the 'right' questions. To do that, we must get back to Dr. Bettelheim and his discussion of what I call 'The Anatomy of a Decision.' As we have said, what we have really been dealing with is the question, "Do I have free will (freedom of choice)?" We have seen that one's attitude toward this philosophical question does have real life consequences. Most of us operate on the assumption that we do have such freedom, although we are seldom aware of such assumption.

Philosophically, the question of free will continues to be compelling. However, in the realm of our everyday choices, the question of whether or not we have free will—freedom of choice—is *irrelevant* because we must act as if there is, and we must accept responsibility for our actions.

But perhaps it is time to concentrate on more important and very relevant questions:

'What is the *process of choice*?' and *'How can we exert more control over making the 'right' choices?'*

My Spectator-self has high hopes that these questions can lead to a more 'scientific' approach to finding better answers.

As stated above, Dr. Bettelheim has attempted to understand the process of choice in a way similar to a physicist trying to determine the path of a ball by analyzing the different factors impinging upon and within it. By altering these factors, the ball's path can be changed. In the same way, by becoming more aware of the factors contributing to our decisions, our actions, can't we try to influence some of these factors to bring about better choices?

I can not help but compare the progress we have made in positively affecting our physical world with the lack of progress in positively affecting the world of human interactions. Understanding the processes of the physical world has led to great technological advances and the potential for a better quality of life. However, understanding the processes underlying human behavior and how we interact with each other—somehow even more elusive—has received less attention beyond the academic and professional worlds, overshadowed instead by superstition and often-unchallenged 'common sense,' with the result that, in our high-speed high-tech new millennium, we have not been able to realize much of the potential for a better world. Hate and blame still dominate. We fight, kill as befits the most primitive societies—only we can now do it globally. In spite of our technological miracles, where is the progress in battling poverty, conflict, wasted lives? We can extend life, but will that life be any more worth living? The promise of a better quality of life still eludes us.

My hope is that asking the right questions—focusing on human behavior and the *process* of choice—can lead us, as individuals and as societies, toward more control over making the 'right' choices.

In simpler terms, Dr. Bettelheim would have wanted us to spend less time judging, blaming others (and ourselves) and more time trying to understand them (and ourselves).

That is the promise of having two lives.

VII

My Rant: Psychology & Technology— Balancing the Scale

The last chapter ended by contrasting the progress made in affecting our physical world with the lack of progress in affecting human behavior and the quality of our human interactions. Now I would like to vent some pent-up frustration.

In fact, be prepared. This is why I'm calling this chapter a rant.

Upon entering a new millennium, it is inevitable to look back on the last one hundred years. Indeed the advances have been awesome. My life would seem like science fiction to my grandparents, and even to my parents. Technology has driven change at an ever-increasing pace until the present Computer/ Internet Age offers boundless promise and potential.

Now here comes the ranting and raving.

I am alarmed, shocked, devastated to see that, with all this progress in technology, we live in a world of undiminished violence and destruction. All of our so-called knowledge has not resulted in a lessening of poverty, war, environmental destruction. Even in the so-called 'First World' countries, so many continue to lead lives of quiet desperation and isolation, hungering for affection, validation.

Two observations before we go on:

#1. **Resentment** and **anger** are still the primary responses permeating human interactions—even in the twenty-first century. Rising to the level of the Spectator is a view shared by a very few.

(Case in point: the election of Donald Trump in 2016. Many voters were hurting and fearful, and feeling abandoned by 'the Establishment.' Their vote was an expression of their valid frustrations. However, they never got past their blame and anger...to understand the reasons behind their frustrations. Acting from rage is seldom in one's own self-interest. I have learned that lesson many times from my own personal behavior.)

#2. Even today, science is often challenged and religion reigns supreme in so much of the world. I cannot help but think of the Dark Ages. The very name tells all. Indeed they were very dark. Great cultures came to an end. No progress; no tolerance; no freedom to create. It was not until the Age of Enlightenment, when science and art again took center stage, that life got better. And most of us would agree that life got better. It seems so obvious.

So I *cannot* understand why that same 'Dark Ages religion' again finds acceptance in this modern world—with the same dark, violent consequences. It is the eighth wonder of the world for me.

On second thought, and on the level of the Spectator, I *can* understand it. Unfortunately, it is actually quite totally explainable—and not some mystifying evil force. However, knowing this does not take away that intense sense of frustration and sadness.

How can this current state of human interactions be acceptable in this new millennium? Why must we waste so much brain power and precious resources just to protect us from each other? On devising ways to kill 'the enemy' or to stop them from killing us? How about 'wasting' more effort just on learning to get along?

Surely, we can do better.

We are allowing technology to build us a wonderful car. But we are focusing on the car—and not the driver. Have *we* evolved along with our material progress? Along with our weapons of destruction? Here we are in the twenty-first century. Yet we are still operating in the primitive survival-of-the-fittest mode: competition, me-vs-you. But there is more to driving than mere survival. We should be paying a lot more attention to the driver. We should be enjoying the ride a whole lot more.

In the relentless march to unlock the basic mysteries of matter, the search to unlock the mysteries of the *mind* and *spirit* have received far less attention—and funding. Apparently it has been easier to understand the force of gravity than the forces of the human mind. Attempts to explain acts of behavior are often dismissed with a glib pronouncement, "Well, it's just human nature. There's nothing we can do about it. We can't change it."

Let's say it like it is. When describing our common nature, jealousy, hate, competition, anger and fear all share equal billing with love, compassion, courage and awe. Each of these components is permanent and will never change. In fact, they are hard-wired to ensure our survival as a species. *So when we talk about influencing human nature, we are not talking about changing human nature or denying any of its attributes. We are talking about creating conditions wherein the more 'positive' human qualities can thrive.* We are talking about magnifying those positive attributes which seem to have been downsized in today's 'modern' world.

In order to influence human nature, we must better understand it. We must break out of old-fashioned ways of thinking and apply a scientific approach, an approach based more on real, empirical evidence.

I guess that's what I've been trying to grapple with in the main themes of my writing. Rather than the theoretical, 'Is there freedom of choice?,' let's actually study how decisions are made. Let's look at the anatomy of a decision under the microscope. Rather than focusing on 'whose fault it is' (and getting lost in labels of 'good, bad and evil'), let's analyze the underlying causes so that perhaps we can influence behavior in the future. Let's come up with new questions for a new millennium.

Maybe we should pause to consider a perhaps latent concern: Do recent attempts to understand the human mind in more scientific terms threaten to undermine the dignity of the human spirit, the soul? My immediate emotional response is, "You bet it does!" It especially makes me crazy to think that thoughts can be altered by changing the balance of chemicals in the brain. But, after a serious struggle with my very indignant self, I really know that my dignity as a human being is not threatened. It's just the same as analyzing the rest of the chemical components of the body. "The whole is qualitatively different than the sum of its parts." The miracle of the human body and mind can never be diminished—or totally explained. Greater understanding leads only to greater appreciation.

To be fair, there *has* been a lot of progress in psychology, recently spearheaded by remarkable advances in brain research technology. Many new discoveries and attitudes in both therapy and drugs have been and are being developed and applied.

As an obvious example, take society's improving approach toward alcoholics. Rather than labeled 'sinners'—shamed and abandoned— alcoholics are now often perceived quite differently and with compassion. Alcoholism is more and more regarded as a disease, with emphasis on treatment, rehabilitation and prevention.

Conflict resolution techniques are being expanded and employed, based on studies revealing the individual's primary need for validation and accommodation. (It's important to note this applies to groups (racial, ethnic...) as well.)

New tools of psychology are constantly being developed. Of course, these may not always prove successful. But it is the same as with theories of matter and energy, which have been and are being constantly changed, rethought and refined. Such efforts in psychology, albeit imperfect, are similarly worthy of our encouragement and support.

My ranting and raving revolves around the fact that these new discoveries in psychology are widely overlooked in the popular conversation. Technology is a magnet for attention. The winds of change are better at carrying the news of the latest iPhone. The question I ask myself over and over again: *Can this new millennium bring real progress in fulfilling the needs of the human mind and spirit?*

Frankly, I have my doubts—and my hopes. Basically, I am a believer in economic determinism. In my own simple meaning, the economic resources and technology, or lack thereof, determine to a great extent the direction a society will take.

Unfortunately, new discoveries in both resources and technology are neither predictable nor controllable. And they are not necessarily user-friendly. These discoveries do not come packaged with compassion or concerns for the human psyche. In today's world they spread globally in an instant, and they come with breath-taking speed. We are always playing catch-up to deal with the changes and challenges they bring. Our political and religious leaders can exert only limited control—which is not to take away from the power they can exert.

On the positive side, however, *the knowledge and technology with which we greet this new millennium is unprecedented.*

So I'd like to end this chapter with a challenge to the forces of technology. It's an idea I've been working on for some time. But I need a little help...

How about coming up with a 'Compassion Pill'? Or, better yet, maybe a chemical that could be distributed in the water supply?

Now that could go a long way to improve human interactions! That could go a long way to balance the scale between Technology and Psychology!

VIII

You Only Live Twice

As you already know, I lead a double life.

Most people know me as Evelyn Aronson, the daughter of my parents. But I have this other 'secret' life, that of the Engaged Spectator.

In this chapter I would like to elaborate on just what it means to live this double life. First I'll try to explain more fully what this second life is all about. Then I'd like to show you how my second life contributes to the first as Observer, Therapist, and Activist (hence, the *Engaged* Spectator). At the end of the chapter, I'll talk about how this second life provides ever-present and satisfying purpose.

I have been leading these two lives for a long, long time, although I didn't fully realize it until later. As I told about in the first chapter, I think it actually started when I was a little girl sitting in temple and reading the prayer book on Friday nights. That's when I remember first becoming aware of a whole world of Being out there—a world in which I was only a tiny, but not unimportant, part.

I read about the "life-giving rains and cooling breezes," "flowering trees and the flowing tide," and the concepts of 'humankind,' 'good,' and 'evil.' And I gradually became conscious of 'the big picture,' the marvelous complexity of Life going on around me and of which I am only minimally aware.

Now I see that I had discovered a whole new world, the domain of the Spectator—the world of my second life. Yes, we all live only twice. And you, too, are leading this double life—a life lived on two levels: the Personal and the Spectator. It is this second world I would now like to explore further with you. For it is this world which has made my personal life so much fuller and rewarding. It is from this world that I have found strength in the face of life's inevitable troubles and suffering.

So how exactly do I lead this double life? On the one hand, I live at the Personal level, as Evelyn Aronson who wakes up every morning and continues to enact her own unique life story. I laugh; I cry; I suffer; I love; I worry; I make choices.

But at the same time, I can watch myself doing these things. I can ascend to the level of the Spectator. And from there, life is totally fascinating, illuminating and non-judgmental.

To show you what I mean, here is a little example.

I remember very vividly in my college days receiving one of those 'Dear Jane' calls, the kind when your boyfriend tells you what a great girl you are—but just *not* for him. As I hung up the phone and the tears began to fall, I recall thinking, "So this is how it feels to get one of those calls." (I'm sure that, if this had been the love of my life, I could never have been that detached.) I proceeded to watch myself react...much like a spectator at a movie. *But at this level the experience was quite interesting and rather enlightening in terms of a chance to study human behavior first hand—and rather pain-free.*

Can you recall similar times when you could observe in a surprisingly objective manner what you were experiencing—sometimes leading to rather unexpected insights?

A rather extreme example of ascending to the Spectator level, which never ceases to amaze and inspire me, comes from one of my favorite cousins. In fact, she is one of my all-time favorite people.

Trudy gave birth to her first child in a small town where medical knowledge and resources were severely limited. The birth was difficult and, midway through, it became apparent that a caesarean section was necessary to save the lives of both mother and child. There was only a minimal supply of anesthetic available, and my cousin was awake through the whole procedure.

"Wasn't it totally awful?" I asked, incredulously.

"Awful? Yes. But, at the same time, it was actually kind of wonderful. I had the chance to watch everything. It was so very, very fascinating!"

I can still see her genuine expression of wonder. (And I can still recall my own sense of wonder at her response.)

She had somehow been able to transform (with the help of the passage of time) her personal tragedy into a life-enhancing experience.

My Cousin Trudy

After relating this incident and introducing Trudy, I think this would be a good time to tell you a more complete version of her story. Trudy is my heroine. She is my ultimate Spectator who could remain at that level when events in her Personal life could have pulled anyone down.

As a result of the difficult birth, her son was left with severe cerebral palsy. She and her husband, Sig, saw to it that Normy had every opportunity. Trudy was barely five feet tall and very petite, yet she somehow managed to get her son in and out of the car to school, lessons, museums and concerts. I could never understand how she did it. She devoted much time and effort supporting his activities and became a highly-valued activist in his school, where everyone knew and loved her.

Normy, unbelievably, went on to become a successful filmmaker, eventually sought out by Hollywood, moving there with his wife and two boys.

And they lived happily ever after.

Not quite. Trudy's life was *not* a fairy tale. Her life was, rather, 'biblical'—taking its storyline more from Job.

Normy died from cancer at the age of forty-three.

Her second son, Robert, was the 'normal' one—smart, good-natured, very conscientious and devoted to his brother. He became a doctor, married a lovely woman, and had an adorable son. Happy ever after? Robert went on to serve in the Army and was stationed at a hospital in Korea which was grievously understaffed. Conditions were bleak and drugs were plentiful. He was plagued by dilemmas of conscience, caught between the needs and confidential admissions of the soldiers in his care and his duty to report all illegal behavior. He became increasingly exhausted and distraught, repeatedly requesting R and R and being denied. Eventually he reached a breaking point, overdosed, and nearly died. (The casualties of war are of infinite variety, and most escape the radar of statistics.) He never really recovered, suffering from debilitating schizophrenia. He divorced, never worked again, and lived with his parents.

He always remained a dedicated son, and Trudy never lost faith in him, never stopped encouraging and supporting him. The two were regularly seen in public, walking arm-in-arm.

At this point one might ask about Trudy's attitude toward life. You would expect self-pity, a turning inward, and a generalized 'life sucks."

But whenever we would meet for lunch, there was a spring to her step and a sparkle in her eyes. She was so alive. After sharing her ongoing troubles (and never denying her deep sadness and daily struggles), the lunch conversation would flow in many directions. She was vitally interested in the news, in the emerging women's movement, in issues and organizations involving social justice, in the beauty and detail of the everyday.

I once went with her to Vogue, a well-known fabric store in Evanston (a suburb of Chicago). She sewed, knit, and crocheted and had a love affair with the color purple. She walked down the aisles as in a church, affectionately stroking the various materials. Finally she stopped at one and held it gently in her hand. Looking up at me, she whispered, "It's so beautiful, it almost makes me cry."

Her Job story wasn't over. In her sixties she had meningitis and lost much of her hearing. True to character, she studied lip-reading and joined an advocacy group for the hearing impaired.

In her seventies she was diagnosed with multiple myeloma and underwent chemotherapy. I'll never forget one particular lunch we had together. I was asking about the effect of the treatment. She leaned over, smiling, as if to confess something. "Actually, Evy, it gives me a 'high.' I kind of feel like I'm tripping."

Spoken like a true Spectator. To me, my cousin perfected the art of living a double life. On the personal level, her life was filled with tragedy and disappointment. But, almost in spite of her life, her 'joie de vivre' remained inextinguishable. As the impersonal observer, her life was full, fueled by an unquenchable curiosity, a genuine compassion, and a sense of holiness in the everyday.

She is my constant inspiration. She holds out my repeated hope that, although our life comes 'wrapped in suffering,' we can still choose to marvel at and enjoy its contents.

Now that you have met my cousin Trudy, you see an extreme example of living one's life on two levels. Trudy's personal life was filled with misfortune and sadness. But, rather than bitterness and withdrawal, she chose to make the most of her second life as the Spectator.

The Spectator as Observer

It has occurred to me that my evolving concept of the Spectator has close parallels to the now popular 'mindfulness movement,' stemming from the teachings of Buddhism, which seriously migrated to the West in the 1970s. This was largely a response to the idealism and spiritual searching of the Vietnam and post-Vietnam years. While formal meditation has not been in my background, descriptions of mindfulness serve to further communicate what I mean by experiencing life as a Spectator.

In the book, *Wherever You Go, There You Are*, Jon Kabat-Zinn writes:

> "Mindfulness has to do above all with attention and awareness, which are universal human qualities. But in our society, we tend to take these capacities for granted and don't think to develop them systematically in the service of self-understanding and wisdom."

And, if I might add, "in the service of appreciation."

Another definition I have heard is that mindfulness is "the act of conscious living"—or "being aware of the miracle of the present moment."

Practicing my own version of mindfulness—trying to be "aware of the miracle of the present moment"—I would like to share some of my 'Spectator moments,' crystallized moments of awareness, hoping you can relate to them. I also hope they will help you recall and stimulate more of your own 'Spectator moments.'

I have already mentioned watching myself react to a rejection phone call from a boyfriend. I've also related my cousin's viewing her own cesarean delivery with fascination. What follows are observations that came to me rather randomly as I became aware of the present moment. You may find these less personal and a little more on the philosophical side.

I had one of those Spectator moments the first time I walked into Whole Foods. I found the store totally overwhelming. It was huge. And when I went to find juice, there were about an infinite number of choices. Then followed the displays of spices, nuts, products from India, Thailand, etc., etc. It was like the whole world had come together in this 'Whole' Foods. Standing there, as a shopper *and* an observer, I was momentarily overcome by the immensity of it. How do my fellow human beings accomplish that?!

Just think about it. And the amazing thing is we *don't* think about it.

On that same order, I sometimes look around my world of things and realize that what I am seeing—and using—are gifts given to me by countless others over countless centuries. Standing in the shower, it's hard to believe how many others are there with me. And I'm not even embarrassed. Think of all those involved in developing and improving: the water system; the heating system; the making of tiles, porcelain, glass, fabric; the soap and shampoo and all the medicines in the medicine cabinet.

That's a lot of people to thank. And I appreciate that shower a lot more!

Now for a totally different type of awareness.

One day I suddenly became aware of...the present becoming the past. A very strange concept, if you truly contemplate it.

I was enjoying one of those ultimate times that you wish would go on forever. It was a special birthday, and my immediate family was gathered around me. I remember feeling so happy and content. Quite suddenly, thanks to my Spectator self, I became aware that what I was experiencing was becoming my past at that very instant. It was like watching the past, a precious memory, in the process of creation.

I try to recapture that insight from time-to-time. It's quite intriguing.

I am often very conscious of going from one level to another—the personal to the observer, and back again.

I must admit it can be a little disconcerting. For instance, I can be in the middle of an argument and just about to make that decisive point when my Spectator-self breaks into an analysis of group dynamics and my place in it. (Is everyone participating? Am I talking too much? Are there personal tensions?...) It's a bit distracting to say the least. But it can be very interesting—and even helpful at times.

Every once in awhile, for no apparent reason, I'll look down at my hand and give the command, "Second finger, rise." And it *does*! And I have no idea how that happens. I become even more aware of how "infinitely much" I'm totally unaware of—and take for granted.

Another conscious moment I often revisit is looking around when I'm part of a crowd. If it's in a restaurant, I look around at the happy faces, the jovial conversations—all those people enjoying life without a care in the world. And then I realize that these people are not much different than I, with their own problems and worries. But for now, in that precious moment, the illusion is thoroughly believable.

Then there's observing an audience in a theater. I begin to think of all the hearts that are beating, all the lungs that are breathing, and the fact that everyone arrived on time, and that the performance, in practically all cases, goes on with the hearts still beating, the lungs still breathing (with maybe an occasional cough). It just boggles my mind. (It also boggles my mind that we simply accept this and do not find it truly awesome.)

As I have grown older, when I meet a friend, I often remind myself how lucky that is. Since I last saw them, think of all the things that have happened to each of us. Think of all the things that could have happened to prevent us from meeting. Yet, here we are, meeting at the same time and place as planned. Isn't that lucky?!

Getting back to the restaurant or theater—or walking down the street, sitting on a train—comes the realization that each and every person (and there are now billions of us!) is the star of their own drama, with their own needs, wants and dreams. Now that's really hard to wrap one's mind around.

I have long been fascinated with 'mind ruts'—the habitual paths our thoughts take when allowed to just drift. I don't know about you, but my thoughts often go over and over the same pathways. I think a lot about my children. I think about my thinking. I often think about my insecurities.

One friend of mine, who is very creative, spends a lot of down time just thinking about new ideas and working them out. That is the path her mind naturally takes.

Another friend of mine thinks a lot about death. The more he tries to not think about it, the deeper the 'ruts' get.

I am exquisitely curious about what other people are thinking—*really* thinking behind their personas. When I 'grow up,' I'd love to do a study mapping out the geography of our mind ruts. I think it would be so fascinating getting to know people from the inside. (I told my idea for such a study to a psychiatrist friend of mine. He said, "That's what I do all day...!")

As a Spectator, other ways of looking at my fellow human beings (myself included) unexpectedly pop into my mind. Sometimes these observations lead me to what I might call different levels of awareness, from what I call the simple to the sublime—even to a 'spiritual high.' Let me describe some of the more memorable ones. They get pretty abstract. See if you can visualize with me.

Sometimes I look around at my fellow human beings and see us as bodies busily fast-forwarding through life—gathering appropriate nutrients to continue the journey.

Then I see each of us as a unique, self-contained world challenged with survival and potential. And that world is miraculously composed of countless functioning parts within parts—organs, tissues—(and that's not even considering the cellular, molecular levels) coordinated by one central brain—functioning almost entirely below the level of consciousness. Totally awesome!

(Now, be prepared. We're going pretty deep—and wide.)

So each of us inhabits our own separate world. Yet we are all interconnected by our similarities to each other and the universal processes we share. And each of our worlds is rotating within the orbits of our family, community, country, world, universe. As individuals, we are affected by and affecting other lives and our environment. We are affected by the past. Our lives, in turn, leave a lasting imprint on the future. Each of us plays a permanent, distinct role in a universal process that is ever-mystifying. We are all part of this eternal Oneness.

It's pretty amazing. And it's pretty amazing to have this gift of consciousness—to be able to appreciate, to some small extent, the wonder of this Life process we are part of. Thinking about it, I get quite a 'religious,' spiritual feeling.

So now we've shared some of my Spectator moments—from the simple to the 'sublime.' I hope by now you understand more fully what I mean by 'Spectator moments.'

And I hope you will enjoy more and more of your own.

Mindfulness—"being aware of the miracle of the present moment."
I guess that's what 'Spectator moments' are all about.

The Spectator as Therapist

Now let's get from the abstract to the more practical. Besides opening us up to a greater awareness, the Spectator can also have an important therapeutic effect on our Personal self.

To illustrate what I mean, I will dare to plunge into marital politics. Over the course of a fifty-plus-year (happy) marriage, a few 'issues' have come up. One incident in particular might serve to make a point.

For no apparent reason our upstairs toilet began to act up. At first there was only a short delay before the tank started refilling after flushing. Then a mild jiggling of the handle would do the trick. Soon a rather prolonged jiggling was required. At this point I brought this problem to my husband's attention. (You can see we had an understood division of labor.)

By the next day, despite his tinkering, it was necessary to remove the entire tank cover and reach in to manually place the rubber plug each time one flushed. Needless to say, I brought this matter to my husband's attention again...and again, with increasing frequency.

This sequence repeated itself over the next couple of days of unsuccessful attempts at repair, until my husband finally lost it, turned to me and exploded with, "Can't you learn how to flush a (expletive) toilet?!!!"

I wilted under the sudden attack. I actually started to go over in my mind how I flushed a toilet and what I might possibly be doing wrong. But then some semblance of reason began returning, and my immediate guilt was replaced by an overwhelming anger at my accuser.

Stalemate. The combatants retired to their corners (while the toilet continued to gurgle).

Several hours later, I was able to withdraw to the comfort zone of the Spectator. I recognized I was dealing with 'a Man from Mars.' Fortunately I had just read *Men Are from Mars, Women Are from Venus,* by John Gray, Ph.D. His words struck a familiar chord.

"Martians value power, competency, efficiency, and achievement. They are always doing things to prove themselves and develop their power and skills. Their sense of self is defined through their ability to achieve results. They experience fulfillment primarily through success and accomplishment."

Armed with this wisdom, I approached my usually mild-mannered partner and asked simply, "Do you feel bad you couldn't fix the toilet?"

"You're (same expletive) right!!!"

And we both began to laugh. (He had read Dr. Gray's book, too.)

Now for the analysis. On the Personal level, I was deeply hurt and felt the innocent victim of senseless anger. I wanted revenge.

But what happened after a while (quite a long while) is that my Spectator-self took over. I started to observe my husband from a more impersonal perspective. In this case, I saw Dr. Gray's 'Man from Mars' earnestly trying to solve my problem but facing the prospect of defeat.

I have found that, when I am able to eliminate myself from the equation, I can often see where my husband is really coming from, and the anger dissolves. Sometimes I even feel sorry for him, and—in the best case scenario—I feel like giving him a cuddle. (But not before he's had a chance to go into his cave to calm down.)

I credit my Spectator-self with a large role in preserving marital harmony.

I'd like to share another example where being the Spectator allowed me to survive in a negative work situation. One of my colleagues, Karen, was extremely difficult to work with. She wanted things her own way, and 'would rather fight than switch.' She was the kind of person who, if you said, "Have a nice day," would fire back, "Don't tell me what to do!" She could be really mean, putting me down, saying 'black' even before I finished saying 'white.'

Her behavior would get me so upset I would go home and yell at my husband, of course. But my Spectator-self was watching above the fray. From that level, it was obvious that Karen was extremely insecure. She suffered from a chronic illness, had had bad experiences with the opposite sex, and was not confident in her physical appearance. To feel important, she needed to put someone else down. That was my diagnosis.

My Spectator-self talked with the Personal me, and I realized that it was not simply her 'fault.' Karen was doing the best she could. From the blame mode I switched to trying to understand her better. Gradually, as she began to feel more accepted by me, she exposed a lighter, sweeter part of her personality. And, after a while, I actually became her friend and confidant. This did not mean that our conflicts in the work situation disappeared. But, more importantly, I didn't take them personally. I knew she was not necessarily reacting to my actions, but in line with her own needs and defenses. I confronted her only when the needs of the students were at stake. (Unfortunately, she had serious troubles with other colleagues, and I would occasionally get in trouble with them for defending her from the wrath she had incurred.) I owe it to my Spectator-self that Karen and I continue to be good friends.

In the section 'Guilt and Parenthood,' we will talk about the lingering resentments we retain toward our parents, and the fact that *we spend most of our lives recovering from our childhood.* As a Spectator in the role of therapist, we may be able to replace some of the residual blame with more healing understanding of just *who* our parents were and *why*. It might make it easier for us to see 'it was not their fault' and 'it was not our fault' either. To come to that insight takes a lot of work. (For some of us, it takes a lot more work!) But the results could be so much worth the effort.

Time for some *self* analysis...lest you think I am off the radar. On a very personal level, I have been known to evoke very negative reactions and responses from my own children. Of course, I always felt the victim to misguided anger and resentments.

After all, I was always trying to be 'good.'

But my Spectator-self, handicapped by a limited perspective, is still able to function to the extent that I can occasionally see how my actions and their motivations might be less than pure. Without going into too much embarrassing detail, one personal characteristic is that I seem to always want to win out in the competition to be 'the good one.' I'm sure you know people like that. They're not easy to take. Especially if it's your mother...or wife.

Following my own theory, we can trace a combination of my DNA and my environment—my innate shyness and need for approval, the praise from my mother, the co-dependence tendencies fostered by my childhood situation, etc., etc., etc.—which resulted in the self-image my family has to deal with. But...*it's not my fault!* And so I thank my family for their admirable attempts at understanding and tolerance.

To sum it up, rising to the level of the Spectator gives one distance from the immediate situation. You see things from different angles—not only your own. It can be a therapeutic view.

I can't keep myself from relating an incident that still makes me laugh when I think about it. Someone taught me a lesson in applying my own words. I was teaching a 'You Only Live Twice' workshop. It was my first time, and this was the final session. And I admitted to the group that I had been really quite nervous about it.

And someone raised her hand to correct me,

"Remember, only one of you was nervous."

The Spectator as Activist—The *Engaged* Spectator

Living a double life, it is interesting to see how each level, the Personal and the Spectator, affect each other. Much of this chapter reflects this inter-relationship. Ironically, while 'Spectator' has a passive connotation, the role actually calls for action. It calls for an *Engaged* Spectator.

This is what I mean. We naturally experience life on the Personal level. Here we have so many things happening to us. We often respond pretty much automatically, conditioned by our past experiences. However, looking at these experiences as the more objective Spectator, we have a better chance to understand what is really going on. The action part comes in when this understanding leads to making 'better' choices, in our personal life and in how we relate to others. Rather than passive victim, the Spectator can help us take more active control.

Seeing our lives from the Spectator's level has broader consequences as well—consequences for how we relate to the larger society we live in. As Spectators, we tend to look more at the 'big picture.' And when we do, we find ourselves considering *our* role in this society.

So when I look at the big picture, what I see is how very dependent we are on one another. I also discover a 'compassion gene' we all share. By acknowledging these undeniable factors, the Spectator demands *action* from its Personal counterpart. Let me show you where I'm going with this.

Let's start at the *very*-big picture level—because that's where I recall a vividly remembered 'a-hah' moment.

Regarding our *interdependence*, I once looked at a chart showing the extinction of species throughout history. It was hard to avoid the dramatic impact of the human march toward progress. Somehow the current endangered species debates (blah...blah...blah) never ignited a gut reaction in me until I saw that one chart. There it was, clearly and undeniably: the strong correlation between changes in human weaponry and use of the land with patterns of extinction. That chart etched an indelible image in my brain. I became acutely aware that one little man, and another little man, and a third little man, each acting over time in his own self-interest (with no evil intent, but armed with the products of his ever-evolving ingenuity) had the power to affect the entire planet.

We are each that one little man. And that power is becoming more and more alarming for the survival of the planet. We are each responsible in our own way for channeling that power.

The above example is a stunning illustration of the impact of one individual's actions even on a global scale. At the more immediate level, this same interdependence obviously exists within our family and friendships, and within the other groups with which we identify: our community, society, etc. So doesn't it follow that our actions—or lack thereof—have real-time consequences? Doesn't it also follow that we have some responsibility to be a positive, *engaged* member of those groups? Because our actions really do matter.

And the *compassion gene*? Being in a movie theater and hearing other people laugh when I laugh, take out their kleenex at the same time, and applaud as one at the end of the story, cements the conclusion that most of us have pretty similar wiring.

In fact, there is a study—by Dr. Jean Decety, reported in the University of Chicago Magazine, April, 2006, entitled "Mirrored Emotion"—of the physiology of empathy, charting its existence using brain imaging. Studies show an overlap in the neural regions that process personal pain and the pain of others. Decety says *empathy* begins with the involuntary 'shared emotion.' He says, "This is something that is hardwired into our brains—the capacity to automatically perceive and share others' feelings."

Shouldn't it be natural to carry that *empathy* exhibited inside the theater into the world outside...and to want to help real people achieve their happy endings?

This realization of our interdependence and our instinct for empathy writes its own agenda. In Judaism there is the concept of "Tikkun Olam"— 'to mend, repair, and transform the world.' The Spectator guides us to observe...and *do*.

What is the purpose of a double life?

I'm thrilled to have the chance to lead two lives. Only we human beings endowed with consciousness can attain the level of the Spectator. As we have seen, the Engaged Spectator is Observer, Therapist, and Activist. Furthermore, as an Engaged Spectator, our Personal lives are provided with a 'built in' purpose that can be achieved to some extent whatever path our lives take.

And just what is this purpose?

From the Spectator's level, as I see it, our purpose is simply *to make the most of our gift of life*: to *know*, to *experience*, and to *contribute* as much as we can... and in so doing, we help others to *know, experience* and *contribute* (and thus enrich our own lives!).

(I will elaborate more fully at a later time—for finding purpose is one of the central aims of this writing.)

By pursuing this purpose, by practicing the art of 'conscious living,' we can always find some degree of meaning and fulfillment.

The Engaged Spectator's role holds out the promise of making our Personal lives—whatever the circumstances—worth living. Aren't we lucky to have two lives?!

IX

What Happened to the Little Girl in the Temple? Marriage, Motherhood, and Beyond

What happened to that 'little girl in the temple'?

My writings began like a personal memoir. So let's go back to the personal part and continue where we left off. But, remember, this is a double-memoir—wherein my Personal life serves up the material for my Spectator-self to try to make sense of. So this will be heavy on the observations, and maybe a little light on the details. With this warning...

I believe the 'little girl in the temple' had grown up and was teaching and going to graduate school in the summers.

One thing in my life was sadly missing, and that was the 'love' factor.

My dating experience had one recurrent theme. Either I liked him, or he liked me. Never the twain seemed to meet.

The good part: according to my philosophy, my Spectator-self had the opportunity to meet and relate (analytically speaking) to all sorts of 'interesting' people.

The bad part: my mother, by this time, was going to the butcher, the baker (literally speaking) and asking if they knew anyone suitable for her daughter.

After all, I was already twenty-five. In those days, that was something for a mother to worry about.

To my rescue came a rather unlikely figure, namely my doctor. This was no ordinary doctor. He was what the medical profession could rightly call a full-service physician. Dr. Manell was an internist who had taken care of me for many years. Besides being embarrassingly good-looking, he was a great doctor. He was not satisfied with just keeping me healthy. He felt responsible for keeping me happy. Somewhere in medical school he must have come across a most unusual job description.

Without my mother's prodding, Doc M. inquired if I'd mind (mind?!) being fixed up with a fellow law student. (I forgot to mention my doctor was going to law school at night and later became an expert in medical jurisprudence, much to the loss of the medical profession.)

That is how I happened to go out on a date with Davy, who spent a good part of the evening talking about his best friend who just started medical school at the age of twenty-eight. All I could think about was how sorry I felt for the poor girl who would marry him.

Three weeks later I got a call from that best friend, whom Davy felt was a better match for me than he was. Two months (and two days) later that best friend and I were engaged.

I might mention that Davy eventually became a highly successful millionaire. I knew he was smart. He knew a good match when he saw one.

Self-Disclosure and Family Secrets

When Neil proposed, it was actually quite unexpected. As I said, we were going together for a short time. I wasn't sure we really knew each other that well—at least I was worried that he really didn't know me.

What I do remember is the overwhelming feeling of happiness and excitement.

At the same time, my Spectator-self was already at work. I was worrying that, if I hesitated with my response, he might always doubt my feelings for him. I knew I had to answer quickly. (Especially since he had already told Davy he was going to propose, and Davy was waiting to congratulate us at his home a few blocks away.)

However, I also felt I had to try to make sure Neil had some idea of what he was getting into. So I suggested we go down by the lake and just talk. Which we did.

It was a beautiful summer day. The sun was shining. The birds were singing. Yet I felt invisible clouds hovering above us.

The two main things I wanted him to be fully aware of had to do with self-disclosure and 'family secrets.'

First, I tried to warn him that I was more serious than he might be prepared for. And I wasn't kidding. (Fifty years later he's still acknowledging that I was right.)

Second, my mother was on my mind. I felt he should know that she was 'different'. She might appear normal, but she really wasn't. And so I tried to elaborate more fully.

Neil listened attentively, acceptingly—assuring me that nothing I had said would make him pause to reconsider.

Feeling I had 'come clean' and he still was determined to go to Davy's with our announcement, I took a breath of relief and enthusiastically said, "Yes!"

The problem is that words go only so far. Experience defines the words unforeseen meaning.

When I told Neil I was serious, little did he know what he was in for. Indeed, 'serious' took on new meaning for him with each successive year of married life. The 'little girl in the temple' was full of 'shoulds,' high ideals, and lots of guilt for when I wasn't following through on my 'should-ing.'

Neil, on the other hand, never took himself so seriously. He didn't live so much in his head. He was multi-dimensional: athletic, creative, spontaneous.

So I managed to weigh him down with new-found and endless responsibilities and obligations. While my part of the bargain was to ease up, enjoy, and be exposed to all sorts of new interests and experiences.

In truth, it proved to be a fair bargain for both of us. Together we shopped the 'shoulds' and 'woulds' and wound up with a full store of experiences and satisfactions—and, luckily, mutual appreciation for our shopping partner's tastes.

Now for the 'family secrets' part. If you have never lived with mental illness, descriptive words are not enough. So, when I tried to describe my mother on that beautiful sunny day by the blue sparkling waters of Lake Michigan, my words were trivialized by the emotions of the moment. It was only later that those words were layered and re-layered with meaning.

After my attempt at full disclosure and going public about our engagement, we just assumed we would get married the following June, giving us a year to really get to know each other. But, much to our surprise, and as a sign of the times (Neil being twenty-eight, and I, twenty-five), both sets of parents independently responded, "Why wait so long?!" We were married in December.

Our first years were a little bumpy as Neil became personally involved in the 'family secrets.'

The wedding was a time of great joy—and relief to our parents. But I never stopped to realize that, for my dad, it proved to be quite traumatic. Not only was he losing a daughter. He was losing a pillar of support in coping with my mom.

Since my mom's 'early retirement' when my sister was born, she continued to develop more psychosomatic symptoms and severe mood swings. While to the outside world her behavior appeared eccentric but normal, day-to-day living with my mom was a constant challenge. We had sought psychiatric help from time-to-time, but with little positive results. Most of the time my dad coped admirably, managing to deny the seriousness of her limitations. He focused successfully on his law practice and real estate ventures, was active in community organizations, was always interested in learning and current events, and enjoyed the respect of family and friends. But there were times when his coping mechanisms malfunctioned and he needed external support.

My marriage took away that immediate source of support—literally, for I had always been living with my parents and sister, as was very usual for girls before they married in those days. (And my sister would soon move away to college.) The first couple of years of our married life sometimes felt to me like a tug-of-war. I would get those dreaded phone calls in the middle of an evening, "Come over right away. Things are bad." And my husband would look at me. I could see the resentment in his eyes. How could he understand the pain and sense of desertion I felt for my dad? How could he understand the nightmare that was my father's life when making that phone call? Yet how could I just get up and leave my husband, my life partner to whom I now owed my primary allegiance? But off I would go.

Fortunately those phone calls weren't often enough to prevent us from enjoying married life. My teacher's salary was sufficient to keep us in the style to which we liked to be accustomed. And so the three remaining years of medical school passed rather happily and quickly. I never felt one bit sorry for 'the poor girl that married him.'

Before long it became time to seek out internships and residencies. Next thing we knew, we were in Cleveland, Ohio, excited and pregnant. What better way to become a good pediatrician (and teacher) than to have your own kids.

An interesting observation on family dynamics: in the three years we spent in Cleveland, we never got one emergency phone call from my dad. Either he didn't want to burden me, or my not being there gave him inner strength. My parents' Cleveland visits with us and eventually our two daughters were so special. The love my mom had shown to me was re-ignited and directed toward her grandchildren. It was these visits, from Neil's parents and my own, that gave us a new appreciation for the institution of grandparenthood. The love and pride of grandparents have the potential to weave a protective cocoon around a child's delicate self-image that can last a lifetime.

And What about My Sister?

Another observation on family dynamics comes as an answer to a question you may have been wondering about. What about my sister? I think her story is very important in illustrating further what I mean about our freedom to make our own choices.

In our last episode, she was still a child—a victim of family circumstances far beyond her control. Much of her behavior had been directed at not doing what my mother wanted her to do. She knew insecurity and guilt intimately. And then something magical happened.

She left the house and went to college—not too long after I got married.

No longer having my mother to bounce off of, she just naturally assumed responsibility for herself. Almost as if overnight, she came into her own. She became extremely self-disciplined. Her study habits could be a model for the student orientation manual. Her room was *neat*. As a student, she excelled. Socially, she was a good, good friend. She finally claimed what had been hers all along. She was smart; she was pretty; she was well-liked; she was fun.

That description carries over to today. She now has a devoted husband, two well-adjusted children with loving spouses, and adoring grandchildren. Contrary to statistics about history repeating itself, she was, and is, a wonderful mother, having learned from her mother what *not* to do and succeeding in not doing it.

My sister is one of my heroes. She is among the few that prove real change is possible. One *can* overcome daunting odds. She is to be admired and emulated.

Her story leads to the consideration of some of the main themes of my writing: *the possibility of change*—and *whether we are free to make our own choices.*

Let's start by taking advantage of our having two lives.

First, on the Personal level, the way we actually experience our lives, my sister made good choices and deserves to be 'admired and emulated' for the positive changes she made.

However, from the perspective of the Spectator (where there is no judging): if her behavior as a child was *not* her fault, can she (or any of us) take full credit for her (our) transformation? Her actions were simply a series of natural responses to her changing circumstances.

This next section is important in illustrating and clarifying my ideas.

The Possibility of Change

Did my sister just suddenly decide to change? Did she one day discover and exercise her willpower muscles?

Before coming to the obvious conclusion that it was up to her, that she had the power within herself to change, aren't we missing an important clue? To quote from above, "She left the house and went to college."

What if she hadn't? What if she had continued to live at home? What if the factors determining her behavior had not been drastically altered?

In a previous chapter we talked about Dr. Bettelheim's attempt to understand human behavior in a way similar to a physicist trying to determine the path of a ball, by analyzing the different factors impinging upon—and within—it. However, human behavior is extremely complex, involving a myriad of genetic and environmental components. It is impossible to predict our actions with anything close to the same precision as knowing which way a ball will roll. However, whether in hindsight or foresight, if a broad enough spectrum of causal factors is known, we can get a pretty good indication of the direction each of us will 'roll.'

Did my sister have the power within herself to change? (Do any of us have this power?) Well, yes—and no. Let's assume our Spectator's viewpoint. In my sister's case, the constellation of causal factors changed. Therefore a new set of responses was called for. *The changes in her behavior were not self-initiated.* She had to react to a completely different environment. After she graduated high school, a new set of choices became necessary. Making those choices, on the Personal level, was experienced as exercising her free will. She is entitled to take credit. She made excellent choices. As a result, her attitude, along with her self-image, underwent a sea-change—from negative to bright positive.

However, let's face it. As Spectators we know that many factors—both internal and external—were in play behind her 'conscious' choices.

Acknowledging that my sister made excellent choices, even those choices did not automatically guarantee a good outcome—and a good attitude. In her favor, genetically, she was gifted. She also *had* received a lot of love and encouragement along the way. The college she picked provided her with immediate social acceptance and a comfortable learning environment. If any of those internal/external factors varied, the outcome could have been very different. Fortunately, the ball was rolled in a good direction.

So let's bump my sister's example up a notch—to the more theoretical. Let's see where we've been heading. We've put her 'free will' decisions and their outcome very briefly under the microscope (superficially studying the 'anatomy' of her decisions). We've looked at her decisions in a similar way to studying which way a ball will roll.

This is a good time to remind ourselves of what is meant by 'the anatomy of a decision' (Part VI). To quote:

> *"Every action we take is the result of an infinite number of intersecting factors coming together at the very moment of decision, only a very few of which are we conscious of. What we will decide will be the sum of all the factors interacting at the exact moment of decision: genetic, environmental, personal, temporal. We really have no choice."*

Yet she *did* choose. Choice is inescapable.

At this point I guess you would agree we have a definite dilemma here. My sister made conscious choices—but she really had no choice at all because of the many factors operating behind those choices. So, what I'm actually saying is that we have no *real* choice.

So where does all this lead? How do we reconcile this dilemma? Again, let's approach this question from each of our lives.

On the Personal level, my sister (and I) can be very proud of the 'choices' she made.

However, studying those choices under the Spectator's microscope, we must admit that—given all the factors operating at the time of each decision—*she could not possibly have done any differently.* I guess, bottom line, our Spectator-self believes in determinism—that what we experience as free will is really inevitable.

My Personal-self really finds this depressing, an affront to the human spirit. After all, what's the use? If we have no real choice, shouldn't we just give up?

But, being lucky to have two lives, we can see that we are dealing with a *false* dilemma.

In our Personal life, we *do* experience consciously the act of making a decision. No matter how we think about it, we cannot escape conscious choice. And we cannot escape the responsibility that comes with our choices. We retain our sense of control.

However, at the same time, in our life as the Spectator, we really know that our decisions are being determined by factors far beyond what we are conscious of.

Why is my Spectator-self not depressed? Well, since these factors are always in flux, our decisions are always susceptible to being influenced. Therefore, this 'determinism' opens a whole range of possibilities for change. We never know what lies ahead.

Rather than depressing, I find a sense of empowerment. Maybe we cannot willfully *initiate* change in ourselves. But we *can* change. And we can provide that outside influence to initiate change in others—or, more ambitiously, in society itself.

In my sister's case, while at home, she was responding naturally to the circumstances of her life. Her responses (often refusing to do what she really might have wanted to do just because that would mean doing what her mother wanted) did not always bring her positive results. It would be so frustrating for me to watch. Nevertheless, she could not respond otherwise. Just as that ball must roll in its determined direction, my sister's direction was set.

More generally, don't we see this all the time? We observe a person acting in a way that to us seems so obviously against their self interest. We say to ourselves, "Why on earth are they doing that?!" And when we earnestly try to help by pointing out the folly of their ways and they don't listen to us, we throw up our hands and dismiss the whole issue with an exasperated, "Well, I tried. Maybe they deserve what they get. They'll never change." Frustration of varying degree is the usual reward for trying to get someone to make that change in behavior. Compassion is the less common response.

One comment I should insert: I have to remind myself that a sense of humility is always a welcome partner. Admitting to a tendency to want to help someone change what I consider negative-for-them behavior, the possibility does exist that I am not always right. And the fact that advice is seldom taken may be a good thing after all!

As long as we're speaking about behavior, I think it's appropriate to include a discussion of *opinions*. After a lifetime of experience, I have concluded that getting a person to change an opinion is like pushing a mountain with your sore left shoulder. You know the feeling. Have you ever had a political discussion and actually changed someone's mind? (Or your own?!) One day, after such a hot and heavy polemic, while licking my wounds, I had a sudden revelation. An opinion *is* like a mountain. It was formed by one's *entire* life's experience. First, there's the layer of parental opinion. Then come the layers formed by the opinions of others, encountered at home, school, work, play...the church, community, media. An opinion is rock-hard and, therefore, deserves patience and deference. However, there is hope—and some evidence—that even an opinion can be changed! (Hopefully for the best.)

From what we have been discussing, we see that change *is* possible. Especially if you believe it is. (In fact, *a positive attitude toward change can be self-fulfilling.*)

Sometimes just a little variation in the balance of circumstances is all that is necessary to change one's choices, attitude—even an opinion.

In my sister's case, the change was major. She moved into a completely different environment, evoking an entirely new set of responses. Happily her responses set her on a new and rewarding course.

Sometimes even a minor event, like a poorly-timed critical remark or just the right word of encouragement can spark a major change in a person's attitude and behavior—depending on the timing or the person's level of receptivity at the moment.

This reminds me of a turning point in my husband's medical career. His internship in pediatrics was very intense. In addition, because of the reputation of the program, his fellow interns were exceptionally competent and had intimidating 'pedigrees'. Being continually sleep-deprived and dealing with extremely sick patients, my husband began to lose his self-confidence and actually started to consider changing his specialty. Fortunately, the head of his department correctly assessed the situation. Dr. Muslin calmly sat back in his chair, put his feet up on the desk, and said, "Neil, I know you will make an excellent pediatrician. Trust me. Just give it some more time."

The end of the story was that his mentor was proven right. That short encounter restored my husband's confidence. And he did become (objectively, of course) a terrific pediatrician.

Another turning point in my own life came when I was working on a project with my school district's superintendent. I was venting my frustration that my teaching took so much of my time but had no impact beyond my own classroom. Thinking back, I have no doubt his reply influenced my subsequent life choices and allowed me to feel more positive about them.

I still remember his words, "Some people are destined to affect a lot of people in a limited way. Others affect maybe a few, but their impact is deep." Thinking back, he influenced a lot of people, but, in my case, the impact was deep.

So, as we have seen, a person's attitude, choices, opinions, although change-resistant, *can* be changed.

Since one's attitude is a major factor in determining which way a person will bounce, it is important to put our attitudes under the same microscope along with our choices. We admire people who have a 'good attitude'. But, rather than taking credit for it, they should feel lucky. What I have come to believe very strongly is that a *positive attitude is a gift,* both genetically and/or environmentally packaged. Some people seem to be born with a positive attitude, no matter what the circumstances. And others have always seen the glass as half empty. Most of us fluctuate. No matter when or how you come to see the glass as half-full, you are lucky indeed.

The moral of my story: *while we are limited in our ability to initiate change in ourselves, we can change. And, as Engaged Spectators, we can at least try to effect change in others (when appropriate)—and even society.* One suggestion: if we arm ourselves with the mantra of low expectations, it will be easier to keep trying. That way we won't be too disappointed—and we might be happily surprised!

Introducing the Children

It's time to return to the beginning of our years in Cleveland where we lived during Neil's internship and residency. Upon arriving there and meeting the new interns, one thing stood out, literally. All the wives were pregnant—including me. (And all the interns were men.)

Pregnancy is an ultimate life experience for a Spectator. All you do is watch and wonder and your body takes complete charge. (With our big and busy brains, how much do we really know about or control our own bodies anyway?)

My husband and I just observed in awe—and kept a now-secret photographic diary.

Neil had one rule for my pregnancy: I could not talk to any other pregnant women about their symptoms. For me, symptoms were highly contagious, and any previously unheard of symptom inevitably became my own.

I did manage to come up with two originals.

By some genetic quirk, I had never lost four of my baby teeth. But in my seventh month, despite years of devoted attachment, these baby teeth suddenly decided to come loose (leading to later major investment in the dental profession!).

Then there was this 'pregnancy tumor'—a little bump on the gums in the front of my mouth. I remember it was a Saturday night and we had invited our good friends for a special prime-rib dinner. (A *very* special dinner, on an intern's salary.) As I took my first delicious bite, a tiny, concentrated stream of blood spurt across the table. My pregnancy tumor had delivered. It took my husband over two hours to admit that, with all his knowledge and training—and accusations of my not believing in him—he really could not stop the bleeding. After a frantic search, we actually found a dentist in the yellow pages who met us in his office at midnight on a Saturday night. Perhaps that is the most amazing part of the story.

When the due date was getting close, everyone in the hospital dining room (where I would meet Neil for dinner on his thirty-six-hours on, twelve-hours off schedule) would ask how I was doing. But after nine-and-a-half months had passed, people stopped asking, and I felt like a curiosity that had long lost its interest. This limbo continued until the beginning of the tenth month (according to our endlessly repeated calculations) when our baby daughter finally decided she was ready to make her grand entrance.

One night I was having stomach cramps. The strange thing was, after 'ten months,' it never occurred to me I might be in labor. I was reading "*The Agony and the Ecstasy"* (truly!) when it finally dawned on me that the cramps came and went every four minutes.

In keeping with my Spectator's perspective, I was always curious about the whole birth process. So I was very lucky to have had a 'normal' labor and delivery, which allowed me to experience natural childbirth—on two levels.

Personally, I was very busy, trying to remember and follow what we learned in birthing classes, concentrating on every contraction, ordering my poor husband around. I was constantly questioning, "Are we almost there?" To tell the truth, I was so busy, I had all but forgotten...the baby. Then finally came that last push, and there she was. I remember looking around the room flooded with sunshine. I felt as if the world itself was born anew. A powerful feeling of grateful elation flowed with the tears.

On the Spectator level, I always wondered what it was *really* like to give birth to a baby. I found myself studying each contraction and the pauses between. I tried to be aware of each stage of delivery. I heard myself moaning, grunting, jabbering—surprising ways to ease the process. Finally in the delivery room, I remember my husband's encouraging, "Now don't forget to look in the mirror." And there I saw a picture similar to the many others in books, magazines and films—only I and *our* baby were in the picture!

Childbirth on two levels balances the natural anxiety and pain with the sense of wonder and fascination. I guess you could call it, 'the agony and the ecstasy'.

The First Child

Just as the Earth was always assumed to occupy the center of the universe, so does the first child occupy that exalted place. Every breath, every (gas-related) smile, and every minute developmental gain are duly noted...and photographed. The best entertainment is just to sit and behold. Everything is to be taken very seriously.

Speaking of serious, when my first daughter was a little baby, I had my books of instruction by my side, my antidotes to free-floating insecurity. For example, when it was time for the first bath, my bath book was open beside me. As I soon found out, this kind of conscientiousness can be carried too far.

One memorable day it was time for a bath. The book said: first, the bath; and second, the feeding. Unfortunately, my daughter couldn't read. So all the while I was preparing the bath, she was screaming in ever-increasing decibels. Then all of a sudden the screaming stopped. I heard nothing. Nothing. I ran to her bedroom to find that, not only had she stopped screaming, she had stopped breathing. Oh, my G-d! I immediately picked her up and frantically started to shake her. (That was before I read the book about the severe dangers of shaking.) Miraculously she started to breathe again. My doctor said this was a breath-holding spell, which sometimes occurs with fright, anger and/or stress, assuring me it was nothing to worry about.

Nothing to worry about?! That's easy for him to say. He's not a new mother—an entirely different species altogether.

This episode had two major consequences. First, book learning had to occasionally defer to common sense, which the shock of motherhood had temporarily anesthetized.

Second, I resolved never to let our daughter cry. Well, that might be an exaggeration, but too much crying became a red flag for me.

As our daughter grew a little older, my husband picked up on this and criticized my 'being too soft'. I started to question this, also. One night there was a showdown. Neil had gone to bed after one of his usual marathon days. I was reading in the living room. All was peaceful...until that first little hint of a cry, which I assumed I had only imagined. Then a second series of undeniable cries intruded into my reality. This time I was resolved to let her 'cry it out'. And cry it out she did. The cries increased in intensity over what seemed like an eternity. Proudly I remained seated, glued to my chair. Finally the cries pierced my heart and I could take it no longer. Reluctantly I got up and moved slowly toward the bedroom door. But I couldn't open it...because my husband had gotten there first!

What about 'being too soft' and spoiling your baby? Dr. Benjamin Spock (who had written the definitive book on child-raising for my generation of mothers), Dr. Neil, and personal observation have contributed to my rather firm belief that the fear of 'spoiling' your baby in the first few months of life is rather overrated. Babies' early reactions usually reflect basic needs. Underlying motives (like bids for attention) await further maturation. That's when child-rearing decisions become a lot more 'challenging.'

Another early memory that stands out is walking with my baby in her buggy down a lovely neighborhood street on a beautiful sunny day. I remember looking down on her angelic sleeping face and being overcome with love. That's the best way I can describe it. I recall thinking, "Nothing shall ever harm you. I will always protect you and your life shall be happy and good."

I deeply believe this is every mother's instinctive prayer when a child is born. Unfortunately life is complicated and we have limited control.

From my newfound perspective as a mother, what most impressed me was the built-in nature of a child's behavior. It was much like watching a bud unfold. There is a certain general developmental timetable to be followed. Yet each blossom has its unique characteristics. And the care given that flower, or lack thereof, exerts its own influence.

I was always led to believe that unconditional love was the key—almost the guarantor of a confident, happy, and well-adjusted child (and adult). But, alas, this belief gives false comfort for the newly parenting. Unconditional love is a worthy goal, but its power is severely limited. This is soon discovered.

When our perfect and perfectly happy baby reached the ripe-old age of eighteen months, she suddenly became very fearful despite all the unconditional love we could come up with. She became frightened of dogs, fire engine sirens—and even Santa Claus. We later found out that 'separation anxiety' (the psychological diagnosis) is common at that age. But, to my husband and myself, it was and will always remain an unsolved mystery, one I imagine many other parents of babies that age continue to ponder.

Then came the inexplicable struggle for independence, better known as 'the terrible twos.' Whenever it was time to do something or go somewhere in a hurry, I would hear those dreaded syllables, "Me, myself. I do it!" From innocent smiles and contented cooing, my sweet child morphed into this strange creature ready to do battle even when there was no apparent conflict.

To put her thirst for independence into a more positive perspective, I would watch with uttermost admiration as our daughter would try to climb those steep hallway stairs—and fall, and try again—and fall, and try again, never giving up until she mastered that new task.

I suppose it was hard for me to understand that, with all our unconditional love and our deep desire to satisfy each and every one of our child's needs, she could still become fearful.

And how could she possibly not want to listen to her parents, whose only wish was to care for and protect her? How could our daughter not want to put on her gloves, or sit in her car seat, or eat broccoli instead of ice cream? Hadn't we done enough to deserve her trust?! Fortunately for her (and, of course, for us—though we hate to admit it), she was smart enough to trade the temptations of security for the challenges of independence. And therein lies the inherent parent-child dilemma.

The Second Addition

Now for some further reflections on parenthood.

Neil and I always wanted two children. We figured that would keep the teams even: two and two. We could handle that.

So, after twenty-two months, our second daughter was born. She was respectful of her due date. But this time I was not ready—at least not completely. I could not leave for the hospital before cleaning behind the toilet because I knew my mother-in-law was coming to take care of our first-born.

This second labor and delivery were entirely different than the first. Everything was on fast-forward. I soon surrendered any control, zooming along on autopilot, on a rather bumpy and, thankfully, short course to a happy and healthy conclusion. One thing was the same: the ecstasy and sense of wonder.

But the same degree of happiness was not distributed equally among all members of our little family. In spite of our attempts to make the big sister enthusiastic about her soon-to-be new companion, the welcome-home scene was a bit tear-stained. She was not exactly excited about sharing her 'exalted place at the center of the universe.' (This point is a foreshadowing of the inevitable discussion of 'place in the family'—which is coming soon.)

I was essentially an only child, since my sister and I are nine-and-one-half years apart. I was totally unprepared for the mighty powers of sibling rivalry. Depending on the particular siblings, symptoms may be obvious or hardly noticeable. In our case, there was that accidental foot in the face, or an occasional loving hug-til-you-cry. In general, though, it was usually more of a 'you do your thing; and I'll do mine.'

One interesting aside: having little children leads to seeing people from a different viewpoint. It's surprising the effect little ones can have on grown-ups. I'll never forget that one day, walking with our two little girls down the street, when an older, rather stern-looking woman approached. She wore a dark suit with a dark, dour face to match. I found myself steering the stroller to the side to avoid any chance of contact. But I could see she was purposely walking straight toward us. Suddenly, her face lit up and her features realigned, producing a great big smile. She stooped down, face-to-face with Marilee and Rosy, and proceeded to make those various silly sounds grown-ups make to elicit reciprocal approval—and, in the process, looking extremely foolish. Then and there I re-learned an important lesson: you can't judge a book by its cover—especially when children are around to expose the sometimes hidden (lovely) contents.

Place in the Family
It's Rigged from the Beginning

Now for that promised and unavoidable discussion of 'place in the family.' Many child psychologists subscribe to the theory that one of the most significant factors determining behavior is a child's place in the family. Statistically, the eldest child tends to be more of an achiever or more assertive. But, as we all know, statistics don't translate easily to 'my child'—or 'your child.' That would be too simple.

Actually, I have come to the realization that the whole system is rigged! As soon as a second child comes onto the scene, the door is open to a whole flood of possibilities. Of course, some are positive, leading to loving feelings and expressions. However, we must acknowledge the whole range of human reactions: jealousy; struggles for attention; guilt; aggression; submissiveness; competitiveness; favoritism; rejection...

It is rare to escape one's childhood without some emotional 'damage.' Whether those scars become assets or liabilities, they leave permanent marks. You can't escape. The system is rigged from the beginning.

In addition to place in the family, there is another related and important feature in this system to consider. Namely, that much of our self-image is formed in these early years—when our Spectator-self is barely functioning. And this self-image, formed by our early interactions with parents, siblings, and others—when we have very limited capacity for fact-checking—has a tendency to stick around. Yes, the system is rigged from the beginning.

Getting back to the importance of place in the family, I already shared about Marilee's reaction to becoming one of two. She certainly wasn't the first older child to have such a reaction, but the specifics of her reaction were still unique to her.

It goes without saying that the first child's personality and behavior have a definite impact on the second. Then again, what that impact is depends on what that second child is like...which then determines the second child's impact on the first. To say nothing of the effect of a third child, or a fourth, etc. To say nothing of the impact of and on the parents...which fluctuates with the family's constantly changing situation. To say nothing of...

Phew! I think I confused myself. Going from the abstract to the more concrete sounds like a very good idea at this point. Let's zero in on just one variable in action.

Our first daughter, true to her gene pool, was very short—very cute, and very short. It was not long before her little sister was looking down on her. It's not rocket science to see this as a potentially behavior-affecting situation.

How she would respond and how her sister would respond—here's the tricky part—hinges on a whole range of factors. Let's throw into the mix their individual temperaments, their physical strengths and weaknesses.

So, how did Marilee respond? How did Rosy respond? How did Marilee respond to Rosy's response? *And* how did we—the omnipresent parental units react? We must not forget to add the response of 'the audience'—the extended family, friends, the stranger on the street. "Oh, honey, is this your big sister?" "Well, *no!*"

Now that I hopefully have raised your curiosity as to how Marilee and Rosy actually danced their duet, I've decided not to go down that road—although family dynamics are always an intriguing read. I'm only going to say that the one variable of shortness that was bestowed upon our first-born put the importance of *place in the family* up front and center.

Logical Consequences

It's time to go back to the books, which I never did put totally aside, in spite of my initial bath/breath-holding trauma. Each parenting generation has their favorite 'how-to-be-a-perfect-parent' guru. When I became a mom, Dr. Benjamin Spock was the dominant figure and had been a household name for some time. He was a positive, reassuring father-figure who encouraged parents to rely on their own intuition and common sense. The bent and wrinkled pages of his book are proof of the countless times I turned to him to restore my peace of mind.

Another favorite of mine was Rudolph Dreikurs. I was especially drawn to his theory of 'logical consequences.' According to my interpretation, he felt 'punishment should fit the crime.' Children should be able to experience the actual consequences of their behavior. For instance, if little Joe sprinkles popcorn artistically over the coffee table and beyond, taking Joe to his room is not exactly connected to his deed. Making him clean up his own mess before he can go on to other things hopefully gives him some clue about consequences.

To show you a personal example of theory in action, let me set the scene. It was a lovely summer's day, and I took Marilee and Rosy to the park for a very fun afternoon. At this particular park, in addition to a great playground, there were animals and a wading pool. A good time was had by all. Until we left.

Prematurely congratulating myself on such a perfect day, I innocently opened the car door. Unknowingly, I had given the signal for battle.

"I want to sit behind mom."

"No, it's my turn to sit there."

"Your turn? It's always your turn. *Move!*"

"I will *not!*"

"Yes, you *will!*"

The battle continued to escalate.

It was time to put theory to the test. Instead of my usual pleading and high-pitched commands, I would try a different tactic—a surprise attack. After all, the books had taught me *there is only one person's behavior I can directly control. And that is my own.* (Unfortunately, that excludes children's and husbands'.) So what I can do is change my own actions, hopefully bringing better consequences.

So I confidently and calmly announced my edict, "I, your mother, am getting out of this car. You will work things out between you. When I see you sitting quietly in your seats, then—and only then—will I return."

True to my promise, I got out of the car and walked some distance away, with the car still in view, expecting to return shortly. I was so proud of myself. I had maintained complete self-control, while at the same time providing a great lesson for my kids in conflict resolution.

I kept watching for the first lull in the fighting and the negotiations to begin. I kept looking. I glanced at my watch. Then I looked again. The battle continued with no signs of a truce. Yet still I continued my quiet vigil, sure of a positive conclusion.

Then, consulting my watch for the umpteenth time, I suddenly remembered we were having company for dinner that night. In the midst of the battle, I had totally forgotten. By now, I was dangerously behind schedule.

Alarm bells went off and panic set in.

I ran to the car, opened the door, and hysterically ordered, "Get in your seats *now!*" Fear was their master. The battle was over. I had lost.

Moral: I still believe in the theory of logical consequences. It *is* valid and *can* work. However, no theory is implemented in a vacuum. Theories give direction, but must be translated into the real world. A parent is not a free agent, always juggling a multitude of pressures. (That's for sure! But that's something our children are seldom aware of, feeling certain our actions are solely reactions to them.) Best intentions 'oft times go astray.' So we do our best—and then we forgive ourselves, as we forgive our children. And resolve to do better another day.

Guilt and Parenthood

A big problem we parents face is guilt. So I feel compelled to return to one of the main themes of my writing, namely: 'Whose fault is it?'

I know that when one of our daughters is having a hard time, experiencing problems, or going through an unhappy period, I cannot escape feeling somehow responsible. My entire history of parenting casts its dubious shadow. What did I do wrong? Was I too protective? Was I not protective enough? Was I too permissive? Was I too critical? At the Personal level, I sometimes feel as if I am drowning in a pool of doubt and self-recrimination. My Spectator-self has seemed to go AWOL.

To give just one example of the hundreds of times I might have done 'wrong,' I'd like to re-open the lock box on our family dynamics. Marilee's shortness posed some interesting challenges. Her sister was always gaining on her, literally looking down on her. Since Neil and I were pretty much tuned into psychological concerns, we worried about Rosy getting too much attention to the detriment of her older sibling. So we suggested that Rosy not seek the limelight at her sister's expense. To this she seemed to agree. Rosy was the kind of child who always went along, never making too much fuss about anything.

Neil and I patted each other on the back. "What insight! What sensitivity!"

What didn't we know...?!

We didn't know how our message was being received by Rosy. It was only years later that we realized how much she continued to hold herself back because of that seemingly insightful intervention.

Occasionally, when Rosy goes through one of those inevitable unhappy times, we fall back into that dark pool of blame. "Why didn't we encourage her to just be herself?" "Why didn't we stay out of it?" "Why didn't we...?"

When my Spectator-self returns and converses with the Personal me, I know deep in my heart that Neil and I were honestly trying to do our best for both girls. We made our decisions after much thought and mostly mutual agreement, constantly re-thinking and re-evaluating. But, in the end, the 'anatomy of our decisions' is complex. We make our decisions based upon the circumstances of the moment—not from the holy heights of hindsight.

Besides, let's face it. How much control does a parent really have over what happens to their children? Fortunately or unfortunately, we are not that all-powerful. Far more factors are at work to determine when our children are happy, or not. As parents, we can't think we're so special.

Thank goodness, with some distance, I do eventually emerge from that black hole of guilt—and know, with reassuring conviction, "It's not my fault."

Disappointingly, so-called rational thinking is not achieved once and for all. There is no guarantee that, with a new situation, I won't fall back into 'depressive' mode. But when I do, when darker emotions again trump reason, I seem to retain a firewall of faith that my Spectator-self will once again prevail. That is my safety net.

In our musings, Neil and I do still wonder what if we had done differently? What if we had told Marilee to hold herself back instead of Rosy? What if we had tried as much as possible not to interfere in any direction? What if? What if? And we always come to a similar conclusion: whatever you *do* do, you're not doing the something other. Whatever you do will have consequences—for better...*or* worse. You never know until looking back from the future. And so we parents soldier on, trying to make the best decisions we can...and that's all we parents can do.

Before our daughter's wedding, my husband and I pondered the question of just how much control we parents really have in the larger scheme of things. We thought about all the things we had done for our 'rose.' The following dialogue (and our toast at the wedding) was what we came up with:

"How to Grow a Perfect Rose"

Mother: How to grow a perfect rose? Let's start with the basics. The raw material. Which, of course, means the genes, which give all the characteristics that make a rose a rose—and special.

Father: I'll take credit for making our rose resilient, and strong.

Mother: What about soft, and sensitive?

Father: And strikingly good-looking, brilliant, intelligent and creative.

Mother: *And modest!*

Father: But no rose grows in a vacuum. So now we must consider the environment.

Mother: First, a rose requires lots of nourishment. So we gave our rose love.

Father: And more love.

Mother: And then—more love.

Father: And a rose also requires understanding.

Mother: So we read about, and studied roses.

Father: And we talked with experts about roses.

Mother: And, frankly, we still don't understand them. (Or her!)

Father: And a rose requires warmth and light. So we kept our rose warm in the winter.

Mother: We even took it to Hawaii in the summer.

And a rose requires constant attention. We cared for our rose, night and day. We talked to her.

Father: She didn't listen.

Mother: We guided her.

Father: She wouldn't go.

Mother: We praised her.

Father: She didn't believe us.

Mother: And we gave her space.

Father: And she took forty-five hundred miles of it.
(She moved to Europe.)

Mother: So now you've heard the basics: heredity, environment.

In conclusion, as parents, on a very serious note, we want to share with you the *single* most important element in raising a perfect rose.

Father: And this can be summed up in a single word.

Both: L U C K !

And that is still our basic conclusion.

When I hear a parent taking credit for his/her child's accomplishments, I involuntarily roll my eyes. Why? Because, looking around at the considerable number of parents and their children I have come upon in my lifetime, I cannot avoid the obvious observations:

Some 'good' parents have 'good' children.

Some 'bad' parents have 'bad' children.

BUT

Some 'bad' parents have 'good' children.

Some 'good' parents have 'bad' children.

So...my main advice to parents (and their children) is, "Be lucky!"

Caveat: This doesn't let us parents off the hook. Because, of course, we know we *do* make a real difference. And *responsibility* is in our job description. So, we try our best—and, if that's not good enough, we just keep trying.

As far as other parents are concerned, I try to follow the Golden Rule, *"Judge unto other parents as ye would have them judge unto you."*

The Concept of Parenthood
There Are No Grown-Ups!

What is a parent? That concept has undergone a lifetime of evolution for me.

Don't you remember when you were little and you looked up to your parents? *They were the original god concept.* They were all-powerful. They could do anything. They were to be loved. They were to be feared. They were to be emulated.

But then my dad wouldn't get me that toy train. Or my mom got mad at me for what I really didn't do. And the mantra began, "It's not fair. It's not fair." My faith in the almighty Parent got a little shaky.

There were times when my dad (my all-loving, all-indulging dad) would actually get angry.

"You should have helped your mother more today."

"Can't you do that right?!

"What's wrong with you?!"

These unhappy times left me with two simultaneous reactions. It was my fault. It was his fault.

As I got older, the 'my fault' part, the guilt part, went underground, taking up more and more space in the subconscious.

But the 'his fault' part was obvious, bearing sour fruits of resentment. Why was he so critical? Why did he get so angry? (I should say that my father was pretty high up on the parental rating scale, so my resentments are more like grapes than watermelons.)

These resentments, distilled from our total childhood experiences, gradually solidify into patterns of blame. "Why am I so self-critical?" "Why aren't I more confident?" "It's because my father—or my mother (or my sister, or brother)—did such and such to me."

This is no simple story with a happy ending. Let's take an honest look. Many of us—in fact, most of us—*spend a good part of the rest of our lives recovering from our childhoods,* wanting an apology for the perceived misdeeds of our parents. If only our parents had not done such and such, we would probably be perfect.

As a child I assumed that my parents' actions were always in response to me. After all, my mom and dad had only one function in life—to be my parents. It was not until much later that I made the amazing discovery that my parents were children of their parents; that my parents had their own lives—their own problems, insecurities and pressures—aside from being my parents.

There was a time when my dad was especially angry with me. I found out much later he was going through some tough economic times. He was edgy; he was irritable. And not because of me. In fact, I should have been jealous to know I was competing for his attention with a host of factors of which I was totally unaware.

The parent as the omnipresent, omniscient god figure gets taken down a peg or two with the passing years.

The real disillusionment came for me when I myself took on the title of 'parent.' When my two little girls looked up at me with their unquestioning, innocent eyes, it's a good thing they didn't know that I had never been a parent before. It was my first time. I was taking my first steps along with theirs.

That's when I came to the startling realization that my parents had been no different than I was now. They had been just as inexperienced, just as insecure, and just as in the middle of their own lives as I was now.

And *that's* when came a second even more startling revelation: *"There are no grown-ups!"*

Now that's kind of a scary thought! But on the other hand, it's kind of exciting, too, because it means that life needs never get boring. As we get older and older, whatever we're doing or experiencing, it's always going to be our 'first time'—our first time to be a grandparent, our first time to be a retiree, our first time to be 'old.' We're always 'growing up.' Our Spectator-selves will always be seeing the world from a new and interesting view.

But one thing remains the same. Our children will always be our children. When they say, "Stop worrying, Mom and Dad. I'm not a child any more," they haven't got a chance. They forgot to read a Parent's Job Description. It's a life sentence.

I remember my ninety-year-old grandma running—er, *walking* up to my sixty-five-year-old father to make sure his coat was fully buttoned. "Harry, it's cold outside!"

Occasionally I have this fantasy that, if we would *start out* as parents and then be 'grow-downs,' we would be such wonderful, understanding children.

One final comment that I think is most important. In dealing with our lingering resentments toward our parents, it may be helpful to try and understand just *who* they were...and *why*. Though this inquiry may present one of the most difficult challenges to our Therapist-Spectator-self, it may also make it easier for us to forgive our parents—like we would like our own children (and others in our lives) to forgive us. *And it would help to replace blame and anger with more healing understanding.*

Observations of a 'Grown-up'

While it may be a little unsettling to realize we live in a world with no grown-ups (although some of us do grow up a lot more than others), as I indicated above, there is a bright side. Life is always an adventure—new perspectives, new developmental tasks. Each new decade brings its own specifications. Each new decade we get to look at ourselves a little differently—as we feel others might be looking at us.

For me, the hardest birthday was number forty. Somehow that loomed very large. You've seen all the 'funny?!' cards about being 'over the hill,' burying your youth, etc., etc. Well, I was so shocked at turning forty that the next year I thought I was forty-two.

I have a friend who was feeling really terrible when she turned forty. She didn't see a doctor because she thought that was the way she was supposed to feel at that advanced age. By the time she did get to a doctor, she was rushed to the hospital. She was actually, medically speaking, in shock.

When I got to number fifty, I realized how young I was at forty. And I had wasted all that time worrying about getting old. Since then I stopped worrying because I knew I was still younger than I would be later. So I better enjoy it now.

I heard an appealing definition of 'old': it's always ten years older than you are. That one works for me.

As I have reached each new decade, it's like I have been climbing these huge stairs, and, with each step up, I can look back upon a new and expanded vista. My life as a Spectator is busier than ever. In the next pages I'd like to share some of my more curious observations with you. I wonder if you'll find them familiar.

Riding the 'Chutes'

When you are younger, you are very absorbed with your own search for identity. The first decade, looking back, lasted an eternity. Many memories remain strongly imprinted—everything a new challenge, a new discovery. The second decade, filled with choices, lasts a little less than eternity. And then things start to speed up—jobs; social-professional circles; relationships. Then come the babies, and we watch the next generation progress through grade school, high school—absorbed in their own search for identity.

But watching these babies—your own, in your extended family, among your friends—become grown-ups, *you begin to see backwards*...from their adult selves to how they got there.

When I was a little girl, there was a popular amusement park called Riverview. A favorite ride was the 'Shoot-the-Chutes.' One of my proudest moments was finally getting up the courage to ride the Chutes. You get into this boat-on-tracks which then proceeds to s-l-o-w-l-y carry you up this steep incline ('mountainous,' from my viewpoint at the time), building suspense with every minute. When you finally, steadily reach the summit, to the beat of your pounding heart, you peer anxiously at what awaits on the other side. Then bravely, swiftly, comes the descent to the waters below—your stomach following close behind.

And that is how, from the perspective of my later decades, I have come to view our life journeys. We start out slowly. Childhood is a gradual ascent, a time wherein our genetic traits gradually reveal themselves amid a changing environmental setting. "He runs so fast!" "She reads already." "He's so friendly." "She gives me such a good argument. I can tell already she'll make a great lawyer."

As we climb higher, both positive and negative traits are encouraged. Or tolerated. Or crushed. These traits become linked to specific plans, careers, dreams. Positive choices are made (between schools, vocational training, military)—or put on hold, or rejected. We are busy getting ready.

And now we're approaching the summit—finally the chance to see where all this preparation—or non-preparation will lead.

But here I see a disconnect. The journey from childhood to adult is so tricky, so long and arduous, that—though I'm fully aware of the ride up, I cannot predict what will happen on the descent. I watch in fascination as, one-after-the-other, each of us 'shoots-the-chutes.'

I went to my thirtieth high school reunion, looking to see what has happened to the 'stars' of the class. Lo and behold, the nerds had become CEO's, while the 'popular kids' seem to have fizzled out. Who knew?!

I felt that my friends, as a whole, tended to be the conscientious-parent types. Of course, all their children were 'brilliant,' 'talented' and 'well-adjusted.'

Let's take a quick inventory, to see how their children's approach to the summit matches their ride down.

Peter: One of my friend's sons, always a serious student, began as a physics major, re-trained in philosophy, and became a professor in a prestigious university in the School of Business. At present he is in a select financial think tank in Manhattan, living with his professor wife and two 'brilliant, talented and well-adjusted' daughters. (No great surprise there.)

Sammy: Then there's Sammy, sweet and sunny Sammy—always very bright, academically successful, with a special talent for figuring out how to make authority figures age quickly! He traded in a surfboard for a competitive executive training program with a major retail giant. He is now a highly-esteemed Rabbi in a very large congregation, supported by his adoring family. (His mother is still in shock—but very happy.)

Louis: What about Louis? He graduated valedictorian of his high school class, with a genius for creative writing. In the midst of a highly desirable graduate program in English literature, he dropped out—because the Vietnam War created a corps of idealists working toward 'the greening of America,' and he decided to join those ranks. Anti-establishment was the creed. His life has since been a series of disappointments, his unrealized potential one of those hidden casualties of war.

Dick: Dick was the son of a workaholic. His father was an abnormally high-achiever, who felt guilty even taking the time to have dinner with his family. So Dick resolved to put family first, dedicating himself to being a devoted husband and father, as well as a successful lawyer. Predictable? Well, almost. For whatever reasons, he has gone through a devastating divorce.

Tom and Jane: I will end with the story of a brother and sister, both meeting our highest standards of brilliance, talent and well-adjustability. Tom is a physician and Jane, a journalist. Both were married with loving children. Both have had their lives unexpectedly turned upside-down by the sudden onset of similar mental disorders.

As John Lennon wrote, "Life happens while we're busy making other plans." Preparation *does* count. That's a no-brainer. Peter and Sammy are proof. Both reaped the benefits of a good family and a solid education. On the other hand,

Louis is an example of just how much our lives are affected by the times we live in. That cannot be exaggerated. Dick was thrown off course by picking a *non*-soulmate. And Tom and Jane unfortunately discovered a shared genetic handicap, activated by periods of high stress in both cases.

Where is the predictability?! When I look back from the future, I said I am reminded of the 'Shoot-the-Chutes.' We ascend carefully, hopefully commandeering all our potential. But when we get to the top, we're on our own. There are no tracks. If we're lucky, we get a great ride and land in a good place. (Actually, we never really land. We're always on our way. The ride never ends...until we get out of the boat.)

There is a bright side to riding the Chutes which we should not overlook. If the ride up is very bumpy—no positive reinforcement, no parental encouragement, no good educational environment—you can still land in a good place.

Lawrence: Lawrence was the son of a single parent. His mom had her own financial and mental challenges. He basically grew up left to his own devices. How did he land? He put himself through law school, began investing in real estate, and eventually became a millionaire and an important player in the gentrification of our city neighborhoods.

This lack of predictability has led me to some new self-advice. It seems that the things we worry about are usually not the things that happen. *So why waste the worry?!* Besides, while we're busy worrying, we may not have time to enjoy what we don't have to worry about in the present.

"How will our daughter do in school? She's shy. She's not reading yet. She's not as fast as the others. The teacher won't understand her. Will she get into a good high school? Can we afford college? I'll miss her so much..."

Meanwhile, she's adorable; she's happy; and she's still at home with you. Like riding the Chutes, it's hard to appreciate how nice the ride is going up, with all there is to enjoy on the way, if you're too focused on what's waiting on the other side. (It's also important to appreciate the ride down, as well, without being too focused on what's waiting for you further ahead.)

Confession: it's not always easy to limit how much worry we waste. And some of us just do have a natural tendency in that direction. (I speak from personal experience.)

To worry or not to worry. That is the question. But, do we really have any control? A conversation I had with my daughter comes to mind. She said there were times when she actually experienced the power to consciously decide what to think about. She became aware of alternative paths for her thoughts to travel along, and she could sometimes more-or-less rationally *will* herself to follow the 'better' path (which, in this case, would mean to detour around the worry).

Following my daughter's lead, occasionally I have tried my own experiments with thought control. And I am happy to report, occasionally it works.

It's Not a Fairy Tale

As I make the climb from decade to decade and look back, I see more and more life stories from the beginning to the end. And I am struck by the fact that there is seldom a real ending. These stories just stop at a good—or a bad—or a somewhere-in-the middle place.

Considering I was brought up on Disney fairy tales with happily-ever-after endings, this observation is quite disturbing. Actually, every book, every short story, every film has a beginning, a middle and an end—happy or sad. In writing classes, the importance of a strong ending is preached ad nauseam. No wonder I find real life so absurd.

Somehow I have managed to keep alive the belief that, given enough time, misunderstandings will be understood, wrongs will be forgiven, enmities will be resolved...relationships will be repaired. This belief stubbornly persists in my heart, but I have long since stopped holding my breath.

My sweet, caring Aunt Jean had a son who lived in California. He had not visited in years. She waited.

"Joey called. He says he's thinking of coming. He says maybe he'll just surprise me and walk in one day." She smiles, sadly.

And then she died. Joey came to the funeral.

Mother-daughter relationships have their own peculiar challenges.

I have a ninety-year-old friend, Kathryn, who has one daughter, Josie. She is haunted by a decision she made over seventy-five years ago.

At the time, the family was living on a farm in the countryside. It was a charming setting—an old stone farmhouse with a beautiful, well-tended garden, surrounded by green rolling fields. Josie was very happy there.

But, as Josie grew older, Kathryn began to worry that her daughter needed more friends and a more stimulating environment. Everyone she knew was recommending a boarding school in the city. Josie tearfully pleaded not to go. But Kathryn, putting aside her own sadness at the approaching separation, and following the urging of her friends, resolved to do 'what was good for her daughter.' She had been assured that Josie would adjust and ultimately thank her for this decision.

As time went on, Josie did not adjust and kept begging her parents to let her come home. Kathryn was terribly upset, figuring she had made an unforgivable mistake. In her desperation, she made an appointment with a psychologist, quite a courageous thing to do at that time. She was advised, in no uncertain terms, that Josie was much better off where she was. So Josie remained in boarding school.

Josie never forgave her mother.

I don't think Josie ever knew the suffering her mother endured during that period or that Kathryn had acted according to professional advice—and against her own deepest feelings.

The emotional separation between mother and daughter has lasted over these long years. I doubt Josie has ever been aware of her mother's lingering pain and remorse—or the yearning for her daughter's understanding and forgiveness. I doubt there will be a happy ending.

Nadia, my friend, has a 'home divorce.' She lives with her husband, Armand, but she does not shop for him or cook for him (each has their own half of the refrigerator), and often does not talk to him. Their marriage of many years has been a cycle of hurt and revenge. There have been interludes of peace and the promise of reconciliation. The latest went something like this:

"Armand, for the first time in many, many years, asked to take me out for my birthday."

(Yours truly, speaking in the voice of eternal hope.) "Wow! That's a good surprise. What did you say?"

"I said *no*."

"No?! Why did you say no?"

"I didn't want him to think he could buy me off. He was just trying to do something material as a way to pay me back for the favor I did the other day. It wasn't coming from his heart. For all he has done to me, he can't get away so easy."

Will there be a happy-ever-after? I fear the story will just stop in a bad place.

The truth is we all seek understanding and validation. We see things from our own perspective—which usually means we know that we are right and we have been wronged. We seek an apology, vindication, revenge, 'justice.' Often we keep waiting...until we die. The problem is we wait for someone who, also, is 'right,' and has been wronged...and is waiting for an apology, vindication, revenge, 'justice.'

It's not a fairy tale. There are seldom any heroes or villains. Good and Evil don't parade on a white and dark horse. There are just people, (countries, tribes...) who are right and have been wronged...and are seeking 'justice.' And we wait... A happy ending? Mostly, there is no ending at all.

Filters

Another symptom of my senior years is that I have become more and more aware of 'filters.' I look around and see that everyone is wearing them. Now I know they've always been there. But somehow they're more noticeable to me than ever.

At first look, I see just naked eyes wide open.

But, upon a closer look, the filters appear.

Just what are these 'filters'? Perhaps I can best describe them as porous lenses that screen what is allowed to pass through and what is blocked out. I think of them as the natural, self-adjusting contact lenses that are formed, unconsciously, in response to the happenings in our lives. These lenses actually determine what parts of reality we let in. Some parts of these lenses grow thicker and less permeable, narrowing our focus and screening out more and more of what doesn't fit into our preconceptions. Some parts thin out, and we become more open to relatively unfiltered input. The process is ever-changing.

What led to my increased awareness of these filters? Perhaps it's a result of having been through one of the most hotly contested primary fights in a presidential election (2008).

It was quite a primary in the historical sense—a woman against an African-American. Both candidates had outstanding credentials, wide popularity, and policies that were not too significantly different. Both candidates, in my opinion, were equally suited to be the standard-bearer of their party.

But soon into the campaign, the divide between the followers in each camp began to widen. Each candidate was elevated to an almost cult status. And that's when I began to notice the filters.

As in any campaign, opposition research was abundant. Past records were distorted, statements taken out of context and blown out of proportion, and the media was awash in insidious innuendoes. But what's new about that?

What was new for me was the willingness of each side to believe in even the most outrageous accusations against the 'other' candidate—even though both were in the same party and advocated similar policies. With each new broadside, I would hear, "I told you he/she was untrustworthy, incapable, too weak, too strong, dangerous..." Yet, when their anointed one was attacked, "It was unfair; just shows how low they can get; it's a total, malicious lie."

It was like each candidate had handed out millions of filters to their supporters. These filters could block out the harmful particles in the airways, leaving only pure sunshine surrounding their candidate.

After a while, regardless of the fact that both candidates were objectively outstanding contenders with similar positions, each side was blind to the worthiness of the other.

I recently read an article by the New York Times columnist, Nicholas D. Kristof, in which he commented on the bitterness of the race and "the resistance to information that doesn't mesh with our preconceived beliefs." He, too, is referring to the unseen filters we are all wearing.

Mr. Kristof went on to cite a study reported by Farhad Manjoo, author of the book, *"True Enough: Learning to Live in a Post-Fact Society."* The study was conducted by Stanford University psychologists among students who either favored or opposed capital punishment. Let me quote Mr. Kristof's description:

"The students were shown the same two studies: one suggested that executions have a deterrent effect that reduces subsequent murders, and the other doubted that.

Whatever their stance, the students found the study that supported their position to be well-conducted and persuasive and the other one to be profoundly flawed."

Kristof went on to say that Mr. Manjoo noticed a rather funny result. Mr. Manjoo wrote, "People in the study became polarized."

Mr. Kristof continues, "A fair reading of the two studies might have led the students to question whether any strong conclusions could be drawn about the deterrence, and thus to tone down their views on the death penalty. But the opposite happened. Students on each side accepted the evidence that conformed to their original views while rejecting the contrary evidence—and so afterward the students on both sides were more passionate and confident than ever of their views."

This study confirmed exactly what I had been painfully and personally experiencing in the day-to-day onslaughts of the campaign. (Of course, my own filter was ready and waiting for this particular study.) You see, I watched a group of friends who have largely enjoyed political harmony over these many years, divide into the two camps. One would outdo the other in vilifying the 'unacceptable' candidate.

The main and very significant differences between the political parties were buried in the polarization between the two camps of the same party.

"I could never bring myself to vote for _____. If he/she gets the nomination, I'll write-in my candidate's name, just to show 'em!"

Asked I, most tactfully, " Do you really mean that? Can't you tell a Donkey from an Elephant?!"

Needless to say, during that primary election many a nice lunch or dinner was spoiled.

It is this event that brought into even sharper focus these filters we are all wearing. The truly fascinating part is we each have our own lenses, starting at birth (or before...). These lenses are constantly adjusted, refined, increased or decreased in strength. The range of our preconceived beliefs and preferences grows larger with our experiences. For some of us, the filters become so strong, that what we see is very limited. For others, the filters remain as thin and porous as possible—able to see reality a little more clearly.

I fear the prescriptions for our filters will be getting stronger and stronger, magnifying the biases and distortions in what we do see. That's because technology gives us more and more power to screen out what we don't want to see. You're interested in sports? There's the sports channel. What about shopping? Lots of choices. If you want to avoid the news entirely, that's really easy, too. If you have a liberal or conservative bias, just find your own channel, radio station, blog, podcast, twitter feed...

We are more able to see what we want to see, while blocking out much of what is going on around us. Unfortunately, what we don't see can really hurt us. I know a lot of people who take pride in not listening to the news. "It's much too upsetting." Yet it is *their* jobs, pensions, benefits that might be lost. And it is *their* children who might get asthma, or won't be able to afford college. We are fortunate to live in a democracy wherein what we do—or don't do—*does* make a difference. 'Filter-lite' is definitely a recommended prescription.

Besides, let's admit it. If we are isolated in our own little worlds, doesn't life get a bit boring? Personally, I prefer my filters thinner. Otherwise I might bore my Spectator-self to death.

The Art of Expectation

I have found a very important mantra to help avoid undue aggravation in one's life. It goes like this:

"Don't expect too much—and be happily surprised."

It's a direct corollary to:

"It's nobody's fault."

And I have two 'case studies' to illustrate this point.

Case #1: Sara is an older woman who came to America from Poland with her husband and five young children when she was in her thirties. She was raised on a farm where life was very primitive. She made her own yarn from sheep's wool and watched her mother use lipstick made from flower-colored butter. Immediately after arriving in her new country she went into survival mode, working full-time while raising her family. Her entire life has been characterized by hard work and care-taking, always going that extra mile for someone else.

Her husband suffered a long, debilitating illness, which eventually necessitated her stopping all outside work in order to provide him with twenty-four/seven care. After he died, she suddenly found herself with no one or nothing to take care of.

From being a strong, healthy woman who never took time for herself, she began to have all kinds of physical ailments and complain about them. I must add that she was already in her early eighties.

Sara has one daughter and four sons. Her daughter, Jane, is extremely devoted, and also extremely busy—working full time, running a household, and worrying about a sick husband. Sara's general unhappiness as well as her physical complaints weigh heavily on her daughter. Anxious to find some solution, Jane concludes that her mom's complaints are mainly caused by a desire for attention and a lack of activity. She tells her mother to volunteer at her church or find other ways to keep busy. She also tells her to spend more time on her appearance—fix her hair, dress more attractively. Jane's strong belief in the psychological importance of looking good was learned from her mother-in-law, whom she very much admired.

Sounds like very good advice. Right?!

But she is dealing with a mother who worked all her life, developed no other interests, and never really assimilated into the modern American way of life. (And, I repeat, she is in her eighties.)

At this point her daughter would be wise to repeat the mantra:

"Don't expect too much—and, possibly, be happily surprised."

and to remember:

"It's not her mother's fault."

Taking the Spectator's perspective, we can see Sara's life experience has not given her tools to deal with her present, very foreign-to-her situation. She is older now, when change is even more difficult. And she has no psychological insight. She *is* coping the best she can.

Although the situation is very frustrating, and solutions are elusive, the anger and resentment which naturally build up take an added toll on the daughter. It might reduce some of the tension to realize it's not her mother's fault. It's not a matter that she *won't* follow her daughter's advice—but that she *can't*.

Maybe, without the anger and the defensiveness it produces, they can better figure out some possible answers. And maybe not. But:

"If she doesn't expect too much, maybe she'll be happily surprised."

Case #2: This story has definite parallels to the first, since we're dealing with someone who is older and retired.

The background: this is about a couple who married later in life, with about a fifteen-year age difference—the husband being the older. Both were serious career people who loved their work and had no intention of ever retiring. Unfortunately, the husband's job was terminated abruptly, and with no recognition of his important long-term contributions to his company. He left with bitterness and unresolved disappointment.

As in Sara's case, he had not developed any outside interests or hobbies. He was set adrift in uncharted waters. The wife, Charlotte, was much younger and continued to work in a very demanding position. At the same time, she was feeling responsible for her husband's adjustment, or non-adjustment, to his new circumstances.

To her great credit, Charlotte was a take-charge person, and actively planned for her husband's daily activities, as well as his medical needs.

The problem was that her husband, Robert, was not similarly self-directed. His relative passivity was a constant irritant. And that passivity spread to the way he followed through with his doctor's instructions.

Needless to say, marital harmony was in serious jeopardy. He just wouldn't do as his wife suggested. And she was only trying to make life better for him.

There is an added dimension to this story. Concerning the medical component, I have noticed differences in attitudes between men and women. It seems that, in general, men's natural approach to medical care is 'denial.' I have personally witnessed this with my husband (who is a physician!). One of my most challenging goals in life is to get my husband to see a doctor. Also, he is not too good at following the doctor's orders. Robert, being a man, follows a similar pattern.

To summarize the situation, Charlotte is facing intractable odds. She sees her husband as deteriorating mentally and physically with no active resistance. Her anger and frustration runneth over.

While there is no way for her to keep the lid on and to not occasionally boil over with resentment, some of that steam can escape by realizing:

"It's not his fault."

At this point in his life, his coping mechanisms are what they are, much weakened by the aging process.

It's certainly not her fault for getting so angry. Not only does it seem he is purposely not trying to do better, but she sees her still-good years slipping away.

However, in the past, she has confided in me that it does help, when she is at her wits end, to remind herself:

"It's not his fault."

And it also helps to:

"Not expect too much—and be happily surprised."

The 'What' and the 'Why'

Certain things that people do—even our closest friends—are kind of 'beyond the usual'...or, at times, really annoying. I think you know what I mean.

A case in point might be people's eating habits. These often give us food to chew on...

Let's take three examples.

I have a friend who has not eaten any meat for decades—even before health, humane, and environmental considerations came into the public consciousness.

I have another friend who is very controlled in what she eats. Her menus at home are carefully planned for their healthy content. Portions are very contained. An occasional indulgence causes quite a bit of anguish. And sweets are a big no-no. In her presence, I am painfully aware of my own less-than-stellar eating decisions.

One day I had a sudden revelation of just how important to each of us is our relationship to eating. And how complex is that history behind our eating habits. Like all attitudes, this relationship has been built up layer by layer over a lifetime. Recently, I began to focus not so much on 'what' that relationship is—but on 'why' that relationship came to be. The results can be very interesting.

Let's start with my meatless friend. This one is unusually straightforward.

When Emily was a little girl living in Mississippi, she was part of a large and poor family. A favorite dish was oxtail soup. One day she innocently asked to have an extra portion of the meat. Evidently this behavior (perhaps because meat was such a precious commodity in the family) was considered unacceptable, and a lesson had to be taught. So Emily was made to remain at the table until she finished the entire oxtail by herself. Needless to say, this traumatic incident influenced her attitude toward meat for her lifetime.

Now let's turn attention to my conscientious friend, Suzie. Her attitudes toward food are not determined by any one outstanding event, which is ultimately true for all of us.

Since I had recently decided to study the anatomy of our eating habits, one day I simply decided to ask her why she thought she paid such close attention to her diet. She thought for a while. Then she remembered, as a little girl, watching her mother going in cycles from uncontrollable eating and gaining weight to periods of 'under-eating' as a recovery balance. This left a lasting impression and surely affected her resolve to maintain control.

However, before I congratulate myself for coming up with an answer to my original inquiry, it's not that simple. Unfortunately, most things aren't. Suzie's observations of her mother are only one part of her relationship to food. Many other factors have influenced her eating habits over the years. And these habits have become deeply intertwined with her identity, with her self image. For all of us, these habits come to reflect not only our attitude toward food—but also our attitude, in some ways, toward ourselves.

Now for that third example, I will look inward. As far as my own eating choices go, there are hardly any foods that I intensely dislike. I am mostly an equal-opportunity eater. So, turning the interrogation process upon myself, I remember an incident from my experience in camp when I was ten-years-old. The main entree for dinner was lima bean pudding.

This particular entree was received with more than the usual camper response of disgust. Then all eyes turned toward me, being seated at one end of the long table. The platter in question was, one camper after the other, passed down to me. Questioning glances followed in my direction. Their expectations were quickly answered, as I enthusiastically chowed down the 'delicious' lima bean pudding. Thinking a little more about that time, I may be one of the few who actually loved camp food and gained weight to prove it.

So what conclusions do I draw from my own experience? Well, for one, I never was what they call a finicky eater. I just liked all kinds of food. Perhaps this was just in my DNA. My mother was pretty lucky in that respect. As far as my other food habits are concerned, they are fun to ponder. But not necessary to this discussion.

We started out by considering things that our friends do that sometimes give us pause. There are lots of other categories that present themselves. One that quickly comes to mind is habits of punctuality—or not.

I remember my mother-in-law telling about her friend who was always late. This very much offended her, and she interpreted the behavior as extremely inconsiderate.

However, as with our eating habits, the behavior is a symptom of many underlying causes. Our relationship to time is very deep and complex. We all know people who are always early; who are always on time; and who are always late. This tends to be another important part of our identity, our self image.

I want to leave this discussion with a fun exercise for you to try. When someone you know has a habit that causes you some irritation, some amusement, some puzzlement, try to figure out where it might have come from. You may not get anywhere with this—and you may wind up far off base. But detective work is always stimulating—as long as you don't take your deductions too seriously.

There is another side benefit. To repeat one of my repeating themes, when I go from judging the 'what' to understanding the 'why,' the actions of the people around us (and ourselves!) are much easier to accept and appreciate.

A Woody Allen Paradox

To paraphrase Woody Allen, sometimes we come to a fork in the road. The one path leads to despair and desolation. The other, to total destruction and ruin. Let us have the wisdom to choose wisely.

I would like to offer a test to help choose wisely when, unlike Woody Allen's scenario, one path just might lead in a better direction—but we're not sure.

The test: *Which way is there more to gain?* (Conversely, which way is there more to lose?)

To show you how it works, let's start with a personal example you may be too familiar with. Sometimes I'm aware that I haven't heard from a friend for a rather long time. It seems to me that I always call her. She never calls me. And I start to become rather annoyed. Should I make that first call? Definitely not. But, after a while it starts to bother me. And I start to wonder if I should be angry...or worried. And if I *should* call.

On the one hand, maybe she doesn't care that much about our friendship. Or maybe she really doesn't want to continue being friends. Or maybe she's not the kind of friend I want.

What to do?
Just not call, and wait to see if she'll call me?

On the other hand, there is the possibility that something is wrong with her. Maybe she is sick, or maybe she is having some kind of a problem.

What to do?
Take pride in hand, and just give her a call?

So now comes my test: Which way is there more to lose (or gain)?

So here is my thinking: If I don't call, maybe now is a time when she needs a good friend. Maybe she is sick. If I'm not there for her, I will feel really bad. But...if I do call, maybe I'll feel bad to know that she isn't thinking about me at all. Applying my rule, I think I'll have more to gain by making the call and knowing that I'm a good friend to her. My pride can handle an occasional blow. Keeps one humble, right?!

And so, I usually break down and make the call.

Now, going from the personal to an issue affecting the broader society, let's take the 'controversial' case of climate change, where the evidence is considered by some to be inconclusive.

On the one hand, it is said *climate change is the result of natural cyclical events*. The variations in temperatures, storm patterns, flooding, and drought represent a normal, unavoidable warming pattern.

What to do?
Not much. Mother Nature is in control.

On the other hand, some say *climate change is in large part caused by human behavior*. There are so many more people, and technology is ever more omnipresent, so that we humans do have a significant effect on the Earth's environment. Regarding climate change, we have increased the amount of carbon dioxide and other greenhouse gases in the air, so more of the sun's energy, in the form of infrared waves, is getting trapped and remaining in the atmosphere.

What to do?
Try to reduce the amount of carbon dioxide and other greenhouse gases.

So we have Woody Allen's 'on the one path' and 'on the other path.' Where do we get the wisdom to choose correctly?

It's time to put this question through my self-improvised test.

So I ask:

Which way do we have less to lose?

(I guess I could put it more positively by asking: which way do we have more to gain? But, in this case, I'm really worried about losing.)

Since we don't know for sure if there is major climate change, and, more importantly, whether or not anything can be done, it does seem that we have less to lose if we operate on the assumption that *there is human-caused climate change.*

In fact, it's a win-win assumption, because we have *everything to gain*—new forms of energy leading to energy independence, less pollution, health benefits, environmental preservation, and new jobs in new industries—while at the same time the earth's climate may remain more stable. *What's to lose?!* (Other than the short-term effects on jobs and profits, an inevitable fallout as societies move forward.)

Let's turn our attention from climate change to another example. Just for fun, let's indulge ourselves by taking on a *really big* question: Can things get better for us humans?

When my husband was a resident at Cleveland General Hospital, he would sometimes be on call in the emergency room with a fellow resident who was from Greece. Now we all know that Greece has a reputation for philosophy. So, true to his Greek heritage, Stefan would engage Neil in deep philosophical conversations at three o'clock in the morning. One topic that came up was whether or not life was getting better. And, ever since then, I think about that question from time to time. I seem to take the same approach as toward climate change.

On the one hand, we have the answer: *This is the way things are, and will always be.* In spite of all our advances, the world is a jungle—wherein we all compete and survival of the fittest prevails. Besides, you can't change human nature.

> What to do?
> Accept the world as it is and do our best to survive.
> "If I don't take care of myself, who will take care of me?"
> "Pull myself up by my own boot straps."

Then there is the worldview that *things can get better*.

> What to do?
> Accept the world as it is. But emphasize cooperation, and try to build social structures that encourage working together to make the world better.

So now let's apply the test:

Which way do we have more to gain?

We must acknowledge we really don't know if the world will ever get more user-friendly, or if whatever we do will make a difference. History keeps repeating itself. War and poverty are a constant. People's inhumanity to each other seems to reach ever new levels of horror. Problems seem to be multiplying on a global scale, and the world looks like an increasingly dangerous place for us humans (and our animal and plant cohabiters).

But what do we have to lose by assuming Life can and is getting better?

To me, again, this seems like a win-win, rather than an either-or. It's hard to see what we have to lose by embracing an optimistic worldview.

Actually, we have no choice. Our innate problem-solving skills and need to live together have always been harnessed to making the world a better place. We can't help it. Medicine, communication, technology and psychology produce more and more tools to help make life better for all of us. *By choosing to believe things can get better, maybe we'll just try a little harder.*

Besides, believing things can get better makes me feel better!

When we get to the question, "Is the glass half full or half empty?"—I'm sure you know where I'm going with that one.

Forever Young

As I shared earlier, growing older often feels like climbing these huge stairs— one step, one decade at a time. With each new step, I have the opportunity to look backward upon a new and expanded vista. Well, now that I have taken a whole lot of steps (and finished a whole lot of decades), I want to take the time to look around where I am, and to contemplate what's ahead. This is what the next two sections are about.

First, let's look around and see where I am.

Gertrude Stein once said, "We are always the same age inside."

As I have grown older, I somehow expected to feel older. Now I'm not talking about the inevitable pains and aches. I'm talking about how I see myself from the inside.

A recent incident put that into sharp perspective. To make my point, I need to first admit to passing the 70th yard line—age-wise, that is. Now let me set the scene.

A group of volunteers I was involved with had gathered in a somewhat disorganized office space. More volunteers had shown up than chairs supplied. The group leader looked around, sized up the crowd, and announced, "Will the younger people stand up so the seniors can have a seat?" Guess who stood up?! Yours truly, of course. It was quite automatic. And I would have remained standing if I had not been stared down. Only then did I realize I had placed myself in the wrong group!

Similar incidents come to mind. We were waiting in a restaurant, and a younger friend offered to give me her seat. "Why?!" I thought. "Is something wrong with me? Does she think I'm too old to stand on my own two feet?!" I politely refused. But she kept repeating the offer, until I found myself on the verge of losing it. Fortunately she gave up the battle just before my anger took visible form.

Once my husband and I were on an airport tram, and the seat offers began. We looked at each other. Did we really look that old? He still looks pretty good to me. Needless to say, the offers were declined with steely coolness.

I feel we are first-class ingrates. We plead guilty to negatively reinforcing the endangered 'respect thy elder' code.

Other troubling incidents occur. We go into a movie theater and request senior tickets. They give them to us...without even a questioning glance. Or we'll see an 'older couple' and realize they're younger than we are.

Now I'd like to talk about my father's experience with getting older. He lived until the ripe old age of ninety-three (although that is becoming more and more common these days). He drove, was working, had a 'girlfriend,' and remained undaunted by those Chicago winter temperatures of you-don't-want-to-know below zero degrees.

Some of my worst winter memories followed that familiar phone call, "Honey, how about taking a nice walk with me?"

"But, Dad, it's f-r-e-e-z-i-n-g out there!!!" Somehow I was never able to ad lib a good enough excuse. (Disclosure: I'm the kind of person who starts wearing gloves in September.)

One day my dad surprised us with a concerned query, "Do you ever have trouble remembering a name?" For us this was a no-brainer, but it seemed to be rather a new experience for him.

This is the same person that I would occasionally accompany to a doctor's office. When the assistant or the doctor came into the room, they would often ignore my father completely and talk directly to me. I would be put in the uncomfortable position of reminding them that *he* was the patient, not I.

Another thing that began to drive me crazy were those inevitable comments, "Oh, is your dad really in his nineties? He's terrific for his age." And my Dad would be standing right there!

Earlier in this chapter I mentioned passing from decade to decade, becoming aware of how society's expectations change with each new decade. The problem is that these external expectations are often not a good fit for a particular individual.

In my father's case, I came to wonder how all these external cues were affecting his own self-image. Thank goodness he was not deterred from accepting his grandchild's occasional challenge to slide down a bannister or two. Hopefully he remained immune to the steady drumbeat of, "You're that old?!"

One definition of 'old' that bears repeating: "Old is always ten years older than you are."

Lately I think a lot about Gertrude Stein's observation, "We're always the same inside." I realize that's not true for everyone, but I know it's true for me. I don't really feel 'older.' When I say my age, it's a surprise to *me*. And I think that's true for many of our friends.

As an aside, I often ponder how people feel in other cultures. My friend's mother came to this country from Iran. She looked old. She wore dark colors, no make-up. Her face was wrinkled and her hair un-styled. I saw no hint of expectation, no desire to explore the possibilities of her new country. Later I was shocked to learn she was only in her fifties. To all outward appearances, she regarded herself, as did her family, as old. But the unasked question remains: how did she feel inside?

The above discussion has led me to some new resolutions in the category of 'do unto others as ye shall want them to do unto you." In the first place, I shall more graciously accept my role in the 'older generation.' As a start, I will try to appear truly appreciative when someone offers their seat or rushes to open that heavy door...before I refuse. Any sign of respect for elders should be positively reinforced.

On the other hand, I resolve not to automatically offer my seat to someone until I'm pretty sure the person really wants me to. I will try to hold off with the complimentary, "You do so well for your age." Most challenging of all, I will try to see past appearances to the person inside.

How do I see myself? In some ways I am still like that 'little girl in the temple.' I see myself as forever young.

Facing the Beyond

Recently a very dear friend's dog died. She took the loss very hard. In truth, the loss of a pet can be as difficult a loss as any. Who else, besides a spouse, is always there? Margaret was in her nineties. You would think by this time she would be used to the loss of loved ones. Obviously, she wasn't. Let's face it. Some things you *never* get used to. She had read some of my writings and noted that I had not dealt with the subject of death. And she lightly suggested I might 'search about' to find some ways of giving and finding comfort. (She was British and had a delightful way of expressing herself.) So that's what I'd like to 'search about' now.

Some sort of comfort? Now that's a challenge. It's a challenge that presents itself more and more as one grows older (if one is lucky enough to have had one's life played out in the normal order of things).

My friend was grieving for her pet. Her dog was her constant companion. The two could be there for each other even with the increasing limitations of age. They provided each other with mutual purpose and pleasure. And now this companion was gone.

But behind my friend's immediate challenge and loss, of course, the larger questions were being asked. How do you deal with the loss of loved ones? How do you deal with your own always-impending death?

Again I turn to Woody Allen to capture my feelings perfectly. To paraphrase, "I don't mind dying. I just don't want to be there when it happens."

Don't you wonder why, if death is such an inherent part of life, it is so hard for us to 'live' with? Why can't we accept the loss of loved ones as we do the end of a day, the passing of summer, the end of adolescence? It's all part of life.

But we humans have a problem. We get emotionally attached. We even get emotionally attached to things. Think...the absence of the Twin Towers from the New York city skyline. Admit it. Don't you still feel a little twinge?

I remember when Senator Ted Kennedy died. How could it be he was no longer a welcome fixture in the Senate? Throughout my life, there have always been certain markers. The Grand Canyon. Beautiful Lake Michigan. The Twin Towers. Ted Kennedy. My cousin Manny. There is this illusion of permanence. But, alas, it is an illusion...that can be suddenly shattered.

In this decade of my life, I reluctantly realize that one of my developmental tasks is to deal with the sickness and/or death of many of those who have always been there—who are a part of my world, a part of me.

One thing strikes me as very strange. While death is an underlying theme in all of our lives, we hardly ever talk about it. Each of us in our own way confronts this ultimate mystery. And yet we don't talk about it very much. (In fact, when you come to think of it, most of our conversations avoid our deepest concerns. We talk about sports, movies, the weather. Probably we talk a lot about other people and what we think of them. We take pleasure and comfort in being with others, usually interacting safely behind our public facades.)

Right now, responding to my friend's query and the fact that loss is taking more space in my life, it's a good time to assume my Spectator's role. From this view, it is fascinating to consider the differing ways we cope...and the variables involved.

Perhaps our *religious* views are one of the main variables. I'm sure you've heard some of your friends express envy for those more religious than they. "I wish I believed in Heaven, in an afterlife, the messiah..." Then you can face death with a certain sense of security—perhaps even looking forward to being reunited with those you have lost. But religious views are varied and deeply held, formed gradually over a lifetime. They are not set by convenience or desire. And they exert a powerful influence on our attitude toward death.

Then there is always the *cultural* variable. Let me tell you a story about my Iranian friend Perry. I think this incident describes pretty well what I mean. I had a friend Milt who Perry had met only once when he was in the hospital. Shortly after they met, Milt died. Perry offered to come to the funeral with me. It was a more-or-less typical funeral according to my experience. Relatives and friends were gathered together in subdued, respectful silence. No one was audibly weeping—except for my friend Perry...who hardly knew him!

To further comment, I have attended funerals for Perry's relatives, and the atmosphere has been anything but subdued. Distraught cries, wails, outward expressions of grief prevailed. Contrast this to the memorial service at the death of President John Kennedy. Jackie Kennedy won high praise for her dignified restraint. "She didn't even cry."

A third variable to be considered is our *individual temperament*. Some of us 'wear our hearts on our sleeves.' Others of us react more 'in our head.' Some are good at hiding feelings. Some worry they have no feelings. Looking back, our temperaments are so different from birth. And they continue to be altered by the impact of life's events.

Religion, culture and temperament all affect our reactions to the death of others. These variables make it possible to generally predict how a particular person will react to someone's death. But the variable of *who* has died can often mock our best predictions.

To each death we bring the baggage of our relationship to that person. And it is usually a 'mixed-bag.' Sometimes the bag is fairly empty—the relationship superficial. At other times we desperately try not to open the bag. We fear its contents. Sometimes the bag bursts open, and we are showered with differing mixtures of love, guilt, sadness, regret, joy.

The death of a spouse evokes powerful, often unpredictable reactions, dictated by the unique circumstances of the relationship. If the marriage has not been exactly stellar, the loss is sometimes easier to take. Often there is a guilty relief. But if the marriage is a good one, the loss can be devastating. Given the choice, I think most of us would rather endure the pain and suffering that comes with losing a partner who has been the true love of their life.

So now we consider what brings us comfort? We each must face that question alone. We each must chart our own course.

This was made so clear to me when my mother died. She was lucky enough to have her life end in an inpatient hospice unit where the family as well as the patient received attentive care. A social worker was always around to give support, to offer the opportunity to vent, to not feel so alone.

Whenever my dad saw the social worker coming, he would practically run in the opposite direction. To him, the social worker became his nemesis. She was a monkey wrench in his coping mechanism. My main job became finding ways to head off that social worker.

And what was that coping mechanism? For my dad, talking about what was happening was not a source of comfort. Quite the opposite. That is not to say my dad didn't talk. He talked about the news, about politics, about his business affairs. He talked a lot. He also walked a lot. His answer was to keep very busy.

When my mom died, there was that time in the funeral home when the family looks inside the coffin to identify the body. Suddenly my dad bent over the coffin and gently, tearfully gave my mother a final kiss. He never said a word.

A few years ago one of my aunts died. Her son was very devoted to her. He was also a very talented writer. In celebration of her death he wrote a poem that has helped me to find acceptance and a certain peace of mind when someone I truly care about dies.

First he reflects on the impermanence of life:

> *"On the glass of my window pain,*
> *Frost paints an evanescent mountain range*
> *Whose jagged peaks rise and plunge in shifting,*

Shrinking patterns, as if I were driving
My auto on a winding road away.

The frost painter and the cloud painter
(If it be one and the same—or if not)
Works in the spirit of the sand painter,
Pursuing no immortal illusions,
But dismissing, without sentiment,
Designs of wondrous intricacy
When the purpose of creation has passed."

But then he offers a lasting vision:

"Frost pictures fade. But for that sublime moment
When sunlight touches them with silver—
For that moment, Rejoice."

Now when I think of my aunt, I do rejoice in the brightness of her spirit that touched so many lives. And that brightness still dims the sadness of her passing.

How else to find comfort? The fact is that people (or pets) really close to you don't disappear. Ted Kennedy, my cousin Manny, they're always really there. In my memories. In the ways they have affected and will continue to affect me. Their presence is permanent. The frost may melt. But the images have lasting consequence.

Sometimes I try a little experiment. I think about my dad. Then I think about how much of the time I was actually with him. Before his last illness, I talked with him probably every day and saw him maybe three times a week. Then there was that period when we lived in Cleveland, and perhaps I saw him once every six months. But, whether I saw him every day or every six months,

I always knew he was there. I always felt his presence and in the back of my mind I knew that he would be thinking about what was going on in my life.

So every once in awhile, I pretend he's still here. I imagine he hasn't died, but I'm just not going to see him today. Because of the power of the imagination, I can temporarily suspend the reality of his death. I can still enjoy his 'presence.' For as long as I live, he will be always be with me. And that gives me comfort.

Switching roles, how do we attempt to bring comfort to others?

Two of my friends suffered (and continue to suffer) through the suicides of their sons. Both of them encountered a yawning, painful vacuum when being with friends. And why was that? They told me it was 'the big elephant in the room' syndrome. There was plenty of conversation—but no one talked about their sons. "Why bring it up? They probably don't want to think about it." But they *do* think about it. They think about it *all the time.* And they want to talk about Steve...about Robert...about what they were like, about their accomplishments, about how much they are missed. And they will never stop thinking about their sons. And wanting to know that you, too, are still thinking about their sons.

So one part of my developmental task is learning how to be sensitive to the particular needs of the one who is grieving. This is indeed difficult. So often we don't know what to say. We feel awkward. We turn to clichés. "He had a long life." (Come to think of it, since when is the pain of loss calculated by age?) "He had a full life." (Better.) "It's good that his suffering is over."

Occasionally we say something stupid. My good friend Anne was widowed when she was very young. It was a very good marriage, and she was left to raise three children on her own. After twenty years of being alone, she married again. This was a second 'love of her life'—and the newlyweds' happiness was contagious to all their family and friends. Two months after their marriage, Richard was diagnosed with cancer and died within the year. At the funeral one of her friends made the brilliant comment, "You're the lucky one. You had two good husbands."

When we're with someone suffering through a loss, maybe it's better to picture they're holding a yellow caution sign. And that sign is to be respected, even if it stays up 'too long'—as far as we're concerned. Trying to be helpful, we advise, "It's time to get on with your life." However, I've come to observe the importance of having the sadness and grieving process fully played out. Each person has their own timetable. And it's very hard to know when it's the right time, if ever, to encourage moving on.

Again, what does it mean to give comfort? For me, that remains a big challenge. Sometimes silence and an understanding glance is all that is needed. Sometimes it's just listening and taking clues from the one in mourning. And sometimes you sense there's a need to talk about the one who has died. Some need to be distracted. Some need to be left alone. *And it's important not to project our own needs onto the person we're trying to be there for.* Giving comfort is a skill we can all practice. Some have a special talent. And, for the rest of us, we try our best.

Besides dealing with the death of others, maybe it's time to contemplate the possibility of our own death. Doesn't it seem miraculous that we are not totally preoccupied with the subject? After all, Death casts its equal-opportunity shadow over us all. But for most of our lives we somehow manage to live outside the shadow and enjoy the sunlight.

How we do this never ceases to amaze me. In fact, we humans have a lot of serious things we could worry about besides dying. We could worry about what might happen to our children, our health, our jobs, our environment... our planet. This worry-business could easily be our full-time job. We could be *paralyzed* with worry. But the wonder is...we aren't. Not if we're 'normal'—although this label does include a wide range of 'worry-ness.' We look forward. We assume the future. We make plans.

As a Spectator we can rather objectively consider how we might approach our own death. Opposite to Woody Allen's wish, we do have to be there when it happens.

Of course, some of us are lucky enough to die rather instantly or in our sleep. A Woody Allen special.

For others, the dance with death can be long or short before the final curtain. Elisabeth Kubler-Ross, in her 1969 book, *"On Death and Dying,"* focused public attention on understanding what it is like to die from the viewpoint of the person who is dying. Her main contribution was to bring awareness and sensitivity to a process which is often ignored or denied.

She outlines 'five stages of grief':

Denial
Anger
Bargaining
      ("Just let me live until my granddaughter's wedding...")
Depression
Acceptance

However, most of us have not read the book. And, even if we have, we don't go through those stages in order. In fact, we may get stuck in any one of them. Our paths are strictly personal. And I'm not sure we know what path we'll take until we're actually on it.

Take Morrie Schwartz, the hero in the widely acclaimed *"Tuesdays with Morrie,"* (written by Mitch Albom, 1997). Diagnosed with Lou Gehrig's disease, he precociously skipped to the stage of 'acceptance' and milked this stage for all it was worth. He was the ultimate Spectator in his dance with death. And so many gained from his performance.

There's my friend, Paula. She has been battling lymphoma for many years. "How do you deal with that Sword of Damocles always poised above your head?"

"Well, honestly, I think I live more intensely. I have a greater sense of appreciation and a desire to fit into each day as much as I possibly can."

My cousin, Lila, was in a fifteen-year struggle with ovarian cancer. We never talked about death. And she went down fighting. She spent her final weeks in the hospital, in constant pain and suffering. The word 'hospice' never passed her lips.

I do have one more story to tell. I recently lost one of my very best friends. She was the one I could really confide in about anything. She had faced a six-year battle with ovarian cancer. I have never encountered a more rational approach to her disease and to her death—and to her life—than I witnessed with Elinor.

Her husband died about the same time as the onset of her cancer. During her first remission, what did she do? She went out and bought a bright red perky little car—and drove it, solo, across country to visit friends and family. She never was one to waste a chance to make her life full and meaningful.

When we would talk about her health status—and she was very open to talking, she would say optimistically, "My doctor has a whole toolbox filled with tools." And, when one tool stopped working, another would be tried.

That is why I was unprepared for the phone call I received one day. Elinor asked my husband and me to come over. She had something to discuss with us.

The discussion went something like this. "I went to the doctor *yesterday*. He told me that his toolbox was empty, and there was nothing more he could really do to keep the cancer in check. So *this morning* I called hospice to arrange for the services I could expect from them. And I wanted to let my friends know of my decision—and I wanted to tell them in person."

It was all matter-of-fact. Little emotion. I could hear the words. It all sounded quite logical. But the meaning was much beyond what I was able to grasp, sitting there as usual, talking with my good friend.

She died a month later. She spent the first part of that month putting her affairs in order, attending her cousin's wedding, going about her daily chores and pleasures. When talking with her, she repeatedly assured me that she had had a very good life and was very grateful. Regarding the 'stages of grief,' she began and ended with Acceptance.

She will always remain an inspiration.

So what is the moral of this story? I guess it is just to applaud all the dancers.

And what about me? Fortunately at this time of my life I have the opportunity to view death from off stage—not as a player but as a Spectator. I am lucky enough not yet to have been given that role, and I honestly do not know how I would play it. I might have some ideas how I *would like* to act. But I am realistic enough to know that when reason, emotions, and pain interact, it's hard to control the performance.

So how do I face the beyond? Since I really don't know what is beyond, I tend to concentrate on the here and now. And try to make the most of it.

Now that you've read this chapter and accompanied me through the decades, I'm wondering if you feel you've learned a great deal about what happened to that 'girl in the temple'? I'm afraid you may be a little disappointed. Not too much in the way of personal revelations. No material for the tabloids. But I did warn you that this was a double-memoir.

Let me explain where this all started. I had been casually writing down some of my 'philosophy-of-life' ideas for a while when one of my daughters happened to find these papers tucked into one of my drawers. "Where did these come from?" she asked. When I told her they came from her mother, she was rather surprised, but quickly recovered with, "Can I show these to my sister and your son-in-law?" Of course, that was fine with me. It's always good to get some attention.

The feedback I got was that what I had written was a little dry and maybe needed to be a more juicy read. Maybe I should not only try to communicate my ideas, but tell the story of how these ideas came to be. Even though this advice was coming from my children, it did sound pretty good. And the timing was perfect, as I had just retired.

So I diligently set out to trace the events in my life to see how they influenced my ideas. And that's what you've been reading.

But now it's time for my personal life to recede into the background. I guess you could say the next part will be narrated more by me as the Spectator.

In the following chapter I want to ask, 'What about God?'—not exactly what you might call light fare. But the question can be quite nutritious. And very relevant in our search to find purpose in our lives, which is one of the main goals of our journeying together. So...soldier on!

X

Going Beyond the God Question

Now it is time to consider more fully the essential question: **How do we find purpose?** Although we may not think about this question directly, or very often, our answers—or lack thereof—do actually determine to a great extent just how 'happy' we are with our lives.

What I really want to know is, even if our personal lives are filled with obstacles and trouble, is it possible to find some sort of fulfillment? Is there some purpose we can all attain?

Let us examine this question as our Spectator-selves. Perhaps our second life can provide us with both the means...and the answer itself.

I have found that finding purpose has a lot to do with how we answer a 'simpler' question: Is there a God? But in this chapter I would like to go beyond that question. Why do I say I'd like to get beyond that question? Actually, this falls into that category of questions I call 'Dead-Enders,' which, as you know by now, I'm not too fond of.

Dead-Enders are questions that often send us on detours around the more important questions we should be asking. We spend too much time on these familiar questions while failing to address those that are more essential and productive.

Two of these Dead-Enders you will find quite familiar. These questions have been dealt with more fully in preceding chapters. Probably a quick summary is not a bad idea before going on to the third. These are:

Whose fault is it?

and

Do we have freedom of will (choice)?

These questions often have all-too-obvious answers. And they lead mostly to blame and guilt.

To the first question regarding fault, our answers ring out loud and clear. "It's his fault!" "It's her fault!" And, of course, there's the reliable, "It's my parents' fault!" "It's the daughter-in-law!" "It's the boss!" "It's the unions!" "It's the Democrats!" "It's the Republicans!" "It's all those politicians!" "It's the government!" "It's the French!" "It's Israel!" "It's the United Nations!"

One thing I know for sure: "It's seldom *my* fault!"

But, as I've come to more fully understand the dysfunctional family dynamics of my own childhood, I have concluded that, in actuality, *"It's nobody's fault."*

That said, it is a natural response to find fault. This is how our Personal-self experiences life. Blame begins early—very early. We get angry at our parents when they can't satisfy our every need. Blame and finding fault are normal, healthy responses.

However, aren't there better questions we could be asking?

Now it's time to benefit from having our second life. Instead of concentrating on "Whose fault is it?", our Spectator-self operates from a more objective perspective and leads us to focus on different questions:

Why do we (and others) do what we do?

and

What can we do about it?

Perhaps these questions can lead us to more fruitful answers.

And then we come to the second Dead-Ender question: *"Is there freedom of will (choice)?"*

For most of us, the immediate answer is, "Of course! Isn't getting through the day just a long series of decisions—most little, some big?" And for those of us who admit to the label 'indecisive,' we are often painfully aware of the process.

A little confession: Sometimes I'm in a restaurant, and I'm faced with the freedom of choice between two entrees. And I'm having trouble deciding. Finally, when the waiter asks for the third time and the moment of decision becomes an imperative, I can't wait to hear what I'm going to say. It's kind of a surprise. (And, after the relief of making the decision, I become sure it was the wrong one!)

But the question of free choice really should go beyond a simple 'yes' or 'no.' Our Spectator-self gives us the opportunity to direct our attention to the whole *process* of choice. Shouldn't we be trying to understand *how* we make choices? Believing that one has complete freedom of will leads to lots of guilt and reinforces our tendency to blame. "It was her choice." "He made bad choices."

In the chapter on 'Graduate School and Freedom of Will,' I discussed the 'the anatomy of a decision.' To briefly summarize, each decision we make is determined by all the factors interacting at the exact moment of decision: genetic, environmental, personal, temporal. So, *consciously*, my Personal-self freely chooses who to vote for. I make a decision. But that decision is the tip of the iceberg. To understand *why* I made that decision, we have to go deep below the surface.

The focus changes from, *"Is there freedom of choice?"* to the more practical question:

How do we make choices?

Perhaps this question can lead to better choices.

And now for the third 'simple' Dead-Ender question, **"Is there a God?"**

Here, too, maybe we need a better question. For, once we begin to debate, "Is there a God?," our discussion breaks down into the "Yes!" and "No!" camps, with multiple sub-groups to be defended...sometimes to the death.

Yet this question is perhaps the central question of all. *It's really the underlying theme of our day-to-day lives.* So please bear with me through this somewhat abstract discussion, because I feel it has most practical implications and will eventually lead us to finding a rewarding and shared purpose in our daily lives.

It frustrates me deeply that much of the conversation on this pivotal subject is spent in non-communication. As I see it, the basic problem is the *concept* of God. *If you define the concept broadly enough—such as 'the source and total of all Being,' most of us would easily agree, "There is a God."*

But the question we're really asking is: *What* is God? That is where the real dialogue starts (and ends). And our individual answers to that question do actually determine a good deal of our own personal everyday choices.

Is God universal, impersonal process? Is God involved in the everyday happenings in the world? Does God show a personal interest in you and me? Are certain types of behavior required by God? Does your concept of God have certain attributes? Just? Merciful? Vengeful? Is God revealed through reason? Is God revealed through revelation? Is our concept of God the 'right' one?

Much of our general attitude toward others—and life itself—actually derives from our concept of God, and the beliefs, assumptions that follow: Are we humans good? Sinful? Is life to be enjoyed? Sacrificed? etc. Our concept of God may be more or less conscious and may express itself as a negative—"There is no God." But, regardless, it is a driving force in the choices we make.

While I have a deep respect for the ways in which we have attempted to answer the question of 'What is God?'—I am concerned now not so much with the answers, but with the divisiveness they bring. Isn't there a better approach—an approach that might help in some way to circumvent the battle of absolutes? Shouldn't it be our goal to avoid our inevitable 'dead ends' and strive for productive dialogue? After all, we have to live together on this one small planet.

(I'm sure we all ask ourselves with the deepest sadness and frustration if religious conflict must forever be our fate—if religious harmony is too difficult an act to produce on this world stage?!)

The approach I'm suggesting as a way to promote respectful dialogue is based on analyzing the *anatomy* of our religious—or non-religious—choices. (Sounds familiar?) How do we come to understand this world we live in? And just what is the human capacity to know God? Let's take our choices under the microscope. Remember, this is an *approach*—and not an attempt at another choice.

Beware. A word of self-disclosure. I think it is necessary to remind you that, according to 'the anatomy of a decision,' my religious choices are the inevitable sum of all the factors (genetic, environmental, personal, temporal, etc.) that have interacted upon my life. And, I guess, in so sharing, I'm attempting to alter the sum of the factors interacting upon your own attitudes toward religion.

My personal search to know God has led me to a serious consideration of our nature as human beings and how we experience life. My college philosophy professor (on whom I had a serious crush and whose words made an unusually strong impression) challenged us to follow Spinoza's timeless direction *to examine the nature of Humankind—as it is in our nature to perceive it.*

What, so far, have I perceived to be built-in to our nature? How do we consciously experience life? How do we *know* anything?

From the privileged view of my Spectator life, my examination has revealed just three basic tools. That's it. There ain't no more!

So this is my diagnosis:

The only tools we have to consciously experience life are our: *Senses, Reason and Emotions.*

These are familiar words. But what do they really mean? Maybe it's time to seriously think about each one. Sometimes we take these 'gifts' for granted. But we are actually speaking of *miracles.*

Senses. For a starter, I experience life through the five basic senses: *I See; I Hear; I Smell; I Touch; I Taste.* Each of these descriptive words is easy to mouth without fully appreciating the magic in their meaning. So that I don't take these gifts for granted, I sometimes pause from my daily routine just to take time to consciously be aware of 'seeing'... 'hearing'... 'smelling'... 'touching'... 'tasting.' (Actually, I've come to call these pauses a *'gratitude ritual.'*)

Nothing serves to focus appreciation more than impairment or loss. I remember being involved in our daughter's homework assignment—to keep her eyes closed for a four-hour period while continuing her regular routine (with a little help from some friends). That was a great assignment, with lasting impact. I also think of our dear friend Hal, a gourmet cook who gradually lost his sense of smell.

Reason. Even more taken for granted, we experience life through our ability to *Know* and to *Reason*, stemming from the gift of *Consciousness*. Life is more than just physical interaction with our surroundings. We attempt to make sense of our interactions—to know what is going on and exercise some control. Perhaps babies first experience life as just a series of physical interactions. And then, as their nervous system develops, they become aware of their surroundings and eventually of themselves, until they finally claim that highest level of consciousness reserved only for our privileged human species.

However, let's not exaggerate just how much we know and/or how much we can control. A bit of humility is certainly due. It's more like navigating among the icebergs, to return to an all-too-appropriate analogy. But this does not take away from our superlative equipment to help us do so.

Emotions. There is a third dimension through which we experience life: our *Emotions*. We do not only sense and know, but we react affectively. From the American Heritage Desk Dictionary comes the definition:

"Emotion: a mental condition marked by excitement or stimulation of the passions or sensibilities, as love, fear, rage, or joy, and often involving physiological changes, as laughter, tears, or nervousness."

Positive emotional responses and little babies seem to go together. (If I previously mentioned a similar incident, I apologize. It seemed to fit in so perfectly, I couldn't resist. And it did happen more than once...)

I'll never forget wheeling our blue-eyed curly-haired baby daughter in her stroller through the crowded aisles of a department store and observing a stern

American-Gothic-type figure coming toward us. Much to my amazement, her botoxed facial features relaxed and rearranged themselves into a full and quite silly smile, and she began to 'kootchy, kootchy' and carry on a dialogue well-suited to our eighteen-month-old daughter.

As an aside, since becoming aware of people's responses to babies, I have been conducting my own little experiment, watching and trying to predict the effects of babies on passersby. It's quite fun and I highly recommend it.

The way we display our emotions continually fascinates. How is it a baby instinctively knows how to cry? A baby's face and my face look pretty much alike when we're crying—or laughing. *A smile is a smile everywhere around the globe.* Excitement, fear...need no translation. Emotions and their overt expressions are built-in. (This is not to overlook the fact that objectively similar situations might bring forth entirely different emotions in different people at different times—and in different cultures.)

I serendipitously came across a project undertaken by the Department of Computer Science at the University of Bath, England, and reported by the BBC News, August 5, 2006. I'd like to quote the summary, illustrating the universality of our emotions:

> "Computer scientists from Bath have helped develop electronic artwork that changes to match the mood of the person who is looking at it.
>
> Using images collected through a web cam, special software recognizes eight key facial features that characterize the emotional state of the viewer.
>
> If the viewer is angry, the colors are dark; if happy, the art appears vibrant.
>
> The project forms part of ongoing research looking to develop a range of advanced artwork tools for use in the computer graphic industry.

'The program analyzes the image for eight facial expressions, such as the position and shape of the mouth, the openness of the eyes, and the angle of the brows, to work out the emotional state of the viewer,' said Dr. John Collomosse from the Department of Computer Science at the University of Bath.

'It does all of this in real time, meaning that, as the viewer's emotions change, the artwork responds accordingly,' explained Dr. Collomosse."

Our emotions, the way we react to our environment, is the third component determining how we experience life.

And now we can return to our question: How do we know?

What we know comes to us through our *Senses,* our *Reason* and our *Emotions.* These are our basic tools for knowing.

And that's it. Yep, there ain't no more.

So How Do We Know God?

Now we're ready for the God part.

Witnessing the birth of a baby...a spectacular sunset...skiing down a snow-capped mountaintop...Haven't you felt that transcendent sense of awe? That moment when *senses, reason* and *emotions* interact to create an experience far beyond the ordinary. There is a sense of wonder, of reverence. For me, and I hope you will agree, I would like to call this a *spiritual,* or a *'religious'* experience.

On the darker side, during the deep blackness of night or in the midst of a violent storm, don't we sense this awe and our own vulnerability? And might we also call this a *spiritual,* a *'religious'* experience—a heightened awareness of forces above and beyond?

I believe these spiritual experiences are universal, and that every society has a spiritual, religious component which comes from deep in our very nature. Sometimes I imagine living in a primitive village in a long-ago time, living completely at the mercy of the forces of nature. My life would be a mixture of vulnerability and awe. No wonder 'religion' evolved, an appeal to the higher powers for some sense of control.

The history of religion reflects this universal spirituality—an inborn sense of awe and reverence, a recognition of the transcendent power of Being. There seems to be a religious 'instinct' that cannot be denied. Every culture has a religious component—if the definition of religion is generously interpreted.

The "American Heritage Desk Dictionary" defines 'religion' as, "The expression of belief in and reverence for a superhuman power or powers."

Let's s-t-r-e-t-c-h this definition a bit to include the 'powers of nature.' Voila! A religious experience and a spiritual experience become one and the same.

There is a universal awareness of the transcendent—a universal 'religious/ spiritual gene.'

It is important to acknowledge this spiritual, religious dimension—a universal striving to live in harmony with those higher forces highlighted by our sense of awe, wonder and fear.

But now for the hard part. This universal striving seems to have produced no universal conclusions. What has this spiritual capacity revealed about the nature of God?

So now we're back to the question of '*What is God?*' And a second question follows: *How do we know?* How do we attempt to answer these questions? What resources can we employ?

Our just-completed foray into human nature has revealed three basic resources at our disposal: our *Senses*, our *Reason*, and our *Emotions*. But these are finite tools, and we are dealing with infinity.

This serious dependency on our limited means of knowing has not seemed to hinder our ability to come up with answers—an almost infinite number of answers when you consider the current number of belief systems, times the eons of years people have been coming up with belief systems since primitive times.

So where does the preponderance of these answers come from? From concepts of God based on *Faith*. In all their variety, each answer offers us an ultimate source of perspective, direction, and meaning as we experience our insignificance and vulnerability in this vast universe. These concepts come to us by 'revelation'—an overwhelming experience wherein an individual bears witness to *divine truth*. These experiences are very real. They cannot be denied. *In matters of revelation, human nature is not equipped to prove or disprove.*

Revelations are to be respected—and/or followed—to the extent that they offer a positive path toward the purpose of life and the ease of suffering. *But not to the extent they justify arbitrarily negating the beliefs of others or inflicting mental or physical harm.*

Herein lies the potential danger of a concept of God based on *Faith*. If the *experience* of revelation is taken as *proof* of revelation, this arms the believer with *absolute* truth. And this leads to non-negotiable and permanent divisiveness among us—often to cruelty and war.

We must respect the obvious limitations of being human. When it comes to knowing the ways of God, *absolute* certainty will forever elude us. We can rely only on the tools of our *senses*, *reason*, and *emotions*—finite in the face of infinity. *We must treat our beliefs with humility.*

One thing I should make perfectly clear: I am making no attempt to deny the existence of God—or the validity or the value of any belief system. That would be sheer unfounded arrogance. *Faith*-based beliefs cannot be denied. Revelation cannot be disproved.

But for the purpose of promoting harmony and dialogue between our differing belief systems, I urge *humility*. I would quote from the Book of Job, "Who am I to know the ways of God?"

Given a broad enough definition of God—such as *'the source and total of all being,'* we can all say, "God."

But if we attempt even one definitive adjective, "God is_____," we are already on shaky ground.

Challenging the possibility of an *absolute* belief in the ways we attempt to define God has consequences that take time to wrap one's mind (and spirit) around. It is important to remember we are not denying the validity of those attempts. We are only confronting our limitations 'to know the ways of God.' It seems, therefore, incumbent upon us *to hold our beliefs with humility*...and some measure of *tolerance* for what others believe to be true.

Accepting our limitations 'to know the ways of God,'—an essential acknowledgement—can serve as a foundation for a more harmonious way for we humans to interact with each other on this small planet.

The Purpose of Life

Now we come to that ultimate question with which we started this chapter. Actually, this is the essential question posed on the very first page of this book.

Is there a purpose we can all share...whatever our religious, spiritual path?

After many years of pondering, I now realize that, whatever was happening in my Personal life, on the level of the Spectator I could always find purpose. This purpose just seemed to naturally reveal itself.

And just what is this purpose? The answer I have come to has a very definite spiritual dimension for me. It is one that can be shared to some extent regardless of one's belief in God.

> No matter what happens in our personal lives, an ever-abiding purpose of life is revealed in the *awareness* of life itself. The purpose of life as my Spectator-self sees it is: **to make the most of this precious gift of life**. *To use our senses, our reason, our emotions—and the physical miracles of our bodies—to know and to experience the awe and wonder that is Life*. To make the most of both of our lives.

To me, this is a purpose within reach. And I will devote the last chapter to exploring more fully how this plays out in the spiritual life we all share.

The Focus on Life—or Death

But first, I would like to bring up a problem I have with many of the organized religions that I sincerely respect. Namely, their focus on death, or their rather narrow focus on what life has to offer.

Considering our shared certainty that we all must die, often in painful circumstances (and to face—*what*?!), it is most understandable that death has become such a focus of religions.

However, focusing one's life on preparing for death—while it may offer comfort and the strength to persist—risks missing out on the gifts of life in the here and now. In spite of our personal challenges, these gifts are always present in the world of the Spectator. It seems that a belief system, while offering the comforting salvation of an afterlife, should also accept a responsibility to direct followers to enjoy their 'God-given' blessings which we *know* exist in this life, and which 'God' has so generously bestowed upon us.

I had the privilege of knowing Ernestine, a wonderful and truly 'religious' person devoted to the church. She was born in Mississippi and spent her adult years in Chicago's inner city. She was extremely poor and personally suffered from the crime, prejudice and violence surrounding her. The church provided a rich and busy (and inexpensive) social life, and, even more importantly, a sense of purpose and the promise of a final reward in the afterlife. Her church designated Ernestine as a healer, and, as such, she felt specially empowered to be a source of comfort and strength to those who needed her. Her religion did bring her self-fulfillment and peace. The value of her religion is beyond question. The validity of her beliefs is not for me to question. I can't even imagine what Ernestine's life would have been like without her church, without her faith.

But I still find myself wishing that her church had provided her with additional support in expanding her Spectator-self's horizons—more deliberately directing her to explore the riches that learning has to offer, including opportunities that might have lifted her out of poverty. In other words, to have encouraged her to more fully live *twice*.

The Problem of Morality

Many feel that religion is a source of morality as well as comfort. It provides a code of ethical behavior. An understandable concern is that, if you take away the fear of God, what happens to morality?

But is religion the only source of morality? Can morality also be based on *reason*?

From the Spectator's view, I believe there is a definite 'yes.'

Once we acknowledge that one of the purposes of life is to make the most of it, we can base morality on *reason*. And our reasoning goes something like this:

Reason leads to a simple observation: making the most of our own life is dependent on the lives of others. Let's face it. We don't live in a vacuum. What is happening to those in our family, our neighborhood, our nation, and—more than ever—the world community, affects every aspect of our daily life. Is our spouse happy? Is our neighborhood safe? Is the air we breathe clean? Do we send our children off to war? The quality of our own life depends upon the quality of the lives around us. Although not always obvious, morality is in our shared self-interest. Doing the 'right thing'—doing unto others what you would have them do unto you—sets off a positive chain of events which ultimately leads to making the most of our own life.

So, hopefully, we have come to see that *morality can be based on self-interest.* And this morality does not depend on—or deny—*faith*. It is a morality based on *reason*. And a morality worthy of any church.

I recently came across a study that supports the theory that morality is actually genetically based. At least when it comes to altruism. This sounds quite intriguing. Right?

Let me quote from a column by Nicholas D. Kristof in the New York Times (January 12, 2010):

> "Brain scans by neuroscientists confirm that altruism carries its own rewards. A team including Dr. Jorge Moll of the National Institutes of Health found that when a research subject was encouraged to think of giving money to a charity, parts of the brain lit up that are normally associated with selfish pleasures like eating or sex.

The implication is that we are hardwired to be altruistic. To put it another way, it's difficult for humans to be truly selfish, for generosity feels so good."

So, whether you believe in God or not, you cannot escape your intrinsic destiny with morality. A morality based on *reason* is genetically backed up!

So hopefully we can end this discussion with an acknowledgement that morality and purpose do not depend only on 'the fear of God.'

Better Questions

So now let us return to our original question: '*Is there a God?*'—or, '*What is God?*' While this Dead-Ender question will continue to challenge us, I believe we can also go beyond it. I'd like to suggest two other questions which have the promise of promoting a more productive dialogue:

What do we know about being human?

and, most importantly,

How would 'God' want us to make the most of our precious gift of life?

Whether one's spirituality is based on *Faith* or on *Reason*, these questions provide a way to explore—*together*—life's purpose, and how our different beliefs and valuable insights can be more universally shared in this modern world, where we have all become neighbors. These questions are what we will deal with in our last chapter.

XI

The Engaged Spectator and the Purpose of Life

The Search for a Universal Form of Prayer

In this final chapter I'd like to explore together how our different religious beliefs and non-beliefs can co-exist and find some common ground. Perhaps there is some form of prayer that we can all say together—a prayer based only on what we know through our senses, reason, and emotions. A prayer that can lead to a fulfilling and guiding purpose in '*both* of our lives.'

As promised, we will not be dealing with the question, 'Is there a God?' We are going beyond that question to consider:

What do we know about being human?

and

How would 'God' want us to make the most of our precious gift of life?'

Let us build on the previous chapter's discussion of human nature and how we experience life. We experience life through our *senses*, our *reason*, and our *emotions*. Occasionally, this combination of *senses*, *reason*, and *emotions* can ignite in a transcendent sense of awe—a *spiritual* experience.

And at this point we understand and recognize that spirituality is a universal component in our nature as human beings.

If this is the case, then how do we provide for the multitude of differing expressions of this spirituality? While many of these expressions are concerned and actively involved with building bridges, we must recognize the present cacophony of warring forces, constantly tearing at the fabric of humanity. In our modern global world—darkened by the shadow of increasingly lethal weapons of mass destruction, the need for our differing beliefs to function in a unified system is as necessary as it is for individuals in a single society to abide by mutually agreed upon principles.

In my 'the world is getting better' idealism, I would wish for the development of a **'spiritual infrastructure'** to accommodate the myriad forms of spiritual expression. The recognition of our universally-shared spirituality would be the foundation on which to build this **'spiritual globalism.'** And, considering our finite means in the face of infinity, that basic framework would be put together with **humility.**

But what is 'spiritual globalism' in more concrete terms? For me, it would start with a prayer we can all say together—the traditionally religious, the humanists, the atheists, the agnostics, the a-theistic—to celebrate our mutual humanity, and to come up with a *universal 'amen'*?

What might such a prayer be like?

I have been thinking about this for a long time—maybe not directly, but always in the back of my mind. And I'd like to present what I've come up with, and what works for me. This prayer is based on the recognition that the life process is so awe-inspiring that—no matter one's belief or non-belief—a prayer of thanks is appropriate and life-enhancing.

And when we pause to be thankful, we become ever more aware of the infinite blessings of life that we all share as human beings. And in this awareness, the purpose of our lives seems to just naturally reveal itself.

The Purpose—and the Prayer

This purpose? Very simply:

To try to make the most of our gift of life.

And just how do we do that? The following prayer is an attempt at an answer. It is based on giving thanks and, in the process, realizing and maximizing our amazing potential. It is a prayer to bring spirituality and purpose into the every day.

A Spectator's Prayer

"I am *thankful* for another day of life.

I am thankful for all the blessings that life brings to us. May I make the most of all these blessings—*as it is in my nature to perceive this 'most.'*

May I **know** *as much as I can,* **experience** *as much as I can, and* **contribute** *to the lives of others so that we can all make the most of this gift of life."*
AMEN

The All-Important Commentary on the Prayer

So what does it mean to make the most of one's life? What does it really mean: *to know; to experience; to contribute.* How do we do that?

Maybe what's called for is to take an inventory of what gifts come with just being a human being? What are our amazing abilities?

We can DO—the ability to *walk, run, dance, draw, write, speak, read, swim, enjoy sexual pleasure, etc., etc.*

We have our SENSES—the ability to *see, hear, smell, taste,* and *touch*

We have our REASON—the ability to *know* and *learn* about:

> *the physical world*—from the smallest particle to the most distant phenomena of space

> *the cultural world*—the history of the past, the complexities of today, and the probabilities of the future

> *the world of 'Me.'*

We have our EMOTIONS—the abillity to experience:

Happiness—to laugh, dance, sing...

Love—to kiss, hug, care for...

Sadness—to weep, comfort...

AWE!

We can CONTRIBUTE—

*And **why** do we contribute?*

(Disclaimer: I don't think people contribute because they are 'good' or 'unselfish.' Basically I believe we all behave in our own self-interest. This stems from our basic instinct to survive. This is one of my Spectator-self's main conclusions. So I have tried to include in my inventory the different reasons *why* we contribute.)

Because:

We just *naturally* want to.
  (...when I see a tiny baby)

It's in the natural order of things.
  (...parents take care of children
  ...men and women are mutually dependent
  ...our abilities and talents satisfy others' needs
  ...we experience empathy and compassion)

We learn more about life.

By contributing to the lives of others, they are better able to contribute to our life.

We feel good about ourself.

Our life becomes *meaningful.*

This 'Spectator's Prayer' reminds me, as my ninety-four-year-old friend says, "Isn't it great to be alive?!?"

XII

One Lifetime—Two Lives! An Ending

As promised in the Introduction, we have been hanging around together on the level of our second lives, the level of the Engaged Spectator, collecting answers and finally confronting *the* question:

What is the purpose of our lives?

After all the serpentining through this personal memoir and reflections, I have gradually come to realize that this purpose is surprisingly self-evident. We have been given the ultimate gift, *Life* itself. And the purpose becomes:

Making the most of this very wondrous gift:

> *knowing* as much as we can;
>> *experiencing* as much as we can;
>>> *contributing* to the lives of others so that we can all make the most of our gift of life.

When you have a gift, you want to make full use of it. You don't want to waste it, not one little bit, if you can help it. That's why it's so great that we have *two* lives to live. By maximizing *both* our lives, skillfully shifting between our personal stories and 'the view from above,' life can be ever-fascinating, challenging and precious... because of, or *in spite of,* the course of our own lives.

The answers collected in the preceding chapters were attempts to search out and magnify obstacles, and pathways, in the pursuit of *making this 'most,'* both as individuals and as societies—because one necessarily depends on the other.

I think one set of obstacles comes from focusing on the 'wrong' questions—or at least, questions that distract and divide us. (Not that these questions are not interesting or important. But, as proven over endless centuries, these questions can never bring universal agreement—not even close.)

As individuals and as societies—and, more and more—as a global society, we are connected by our similarities and our interdependence. I strongly believe it is more important than ever that we focus on the basic questions that can bring us together:

Rather than:

> *Whose fault is it?*
>
> *(It's nobody's fault!)*

Let's ask:

> *Why do we do what we do?*
>
> *What can we do about it?*

Rather than:

> *Is their freedom of will (choice)?*

Let's ask:

> *What is the process of choice?*

How can we exert more control over making the right choices?

Rather than:

Is there a God?

Let's ask:

How would 'God' want us to make the most of our precious gift of life?

We have explored how our basic assumptions regarding 'Fault,' 'Free Will,' and 'God' actually do affect every aspect of our lives. By becoming aware of our own personal assumptions and those of our greater community, and by holding them up to the light of humility and compassion, we can perhaps find our way toward more harmony and fulfillment by asking those more practical and constructive questions.

So, in this final chapter, let's turn to: *How would 'God' want us to make the most of our precious gift of life?*

As I see it, if we have been given a gift, I believe the giver would want us to make the most of it. Considering pathways to make this 'most,' if I were to write a "Guide to a Double Life," the need to weave awareness rituals into the fabric of daily life would be right up there. After all, each new day really *is* a miracle. We can see. We can love. We can do. Starting out each day with a prayer (or affirmation) just to consciously acknowledge this new day works for me. Some mornings I actually take time to marvel when nothing hurts. Think of the infinite possibilities—of all the parts of our bodies that are taking quite good care of themselves. I try to remember not to take each meal for granted. Sometimes, when I meet a friend, I start to think of all that has happened—and could have happened—to each of us since we last met. Isn't it quite wonderful I get to see them again?!

I believe 'Appreciation Ritual' is a key to leading a successful double life. It shifts one back and forth from the Personal to the Spectator. The art of 'conscious living' can constantly remind us of the ever-present gifts life offers, even when our personal lives are deeply troubled.

Remember, we are not wearing rosy-colored glasses. As brought out in previous chapters, life is *not* an unqualified gift. It is wrapped in suffering, sickness and cruelty. Life is not user-friendly. Nature and human nature have tragic dark sides.

Nonetheless, *we must not lose that transcendent awe of the life process itself and our potential to partake.*

A word of caution: our natural desire to find purpose can lead to increasing frustration at the Personal level. "I don't have an all-consuming passion." "I don't have the time or freedom to really pursue my own goals." "I'm not going to save the world or write the next best seller." "My life is not important. I have nothing to offer." "I have no strong direction to my life."

There is an additional, more forgiving way to measure one's purpose—more easily within our control, equally valid and always attainable on a day-to-day basis. When the Personal me is caught in a downward spiral of negativity, and everything seems to be going wrong (you know the script...), I can remind myself that "only one of us is having a bad day." My Spectator-self is still available to *make the most of this day.* I can ask myself:

*Am I **using** the gifts of life?*

Am I knowing, learning?

Am I experiencing (physically, mentally, emotionally, spiritually)?

Am I *contributing* to the lives of others?

If I can answer 'yes' to *any* of these questions, my Personal-self has the satisfaction of knowing my day has been meaningful.

My Personal-self—My Spectator-self. One lifetime—two lives!

About the Author

Evelyn Aronson has had a lifelong passion for making the most of life, this wonderful gift that we must not take for granted.

After attending undergraduate school at Northwestern University, she received her master's degree from the University of Chicago. She was a teacher for over thirty years, teaching in diverse educational settings. She was honored with the first Outstanding Teacher of the Year Award from Skokie District 68, in Skokie, Illinois. More recently, she taught at the Lifelong Learning Institute at National-Louis University and the Beth Emet Institute of Adult Studies.

Aronson and her husband, a retired pediatrician, have two adult daughters, both of whom are doctors of psychology.